# Old Companions

*Grey Scale and Black Line Colouring*

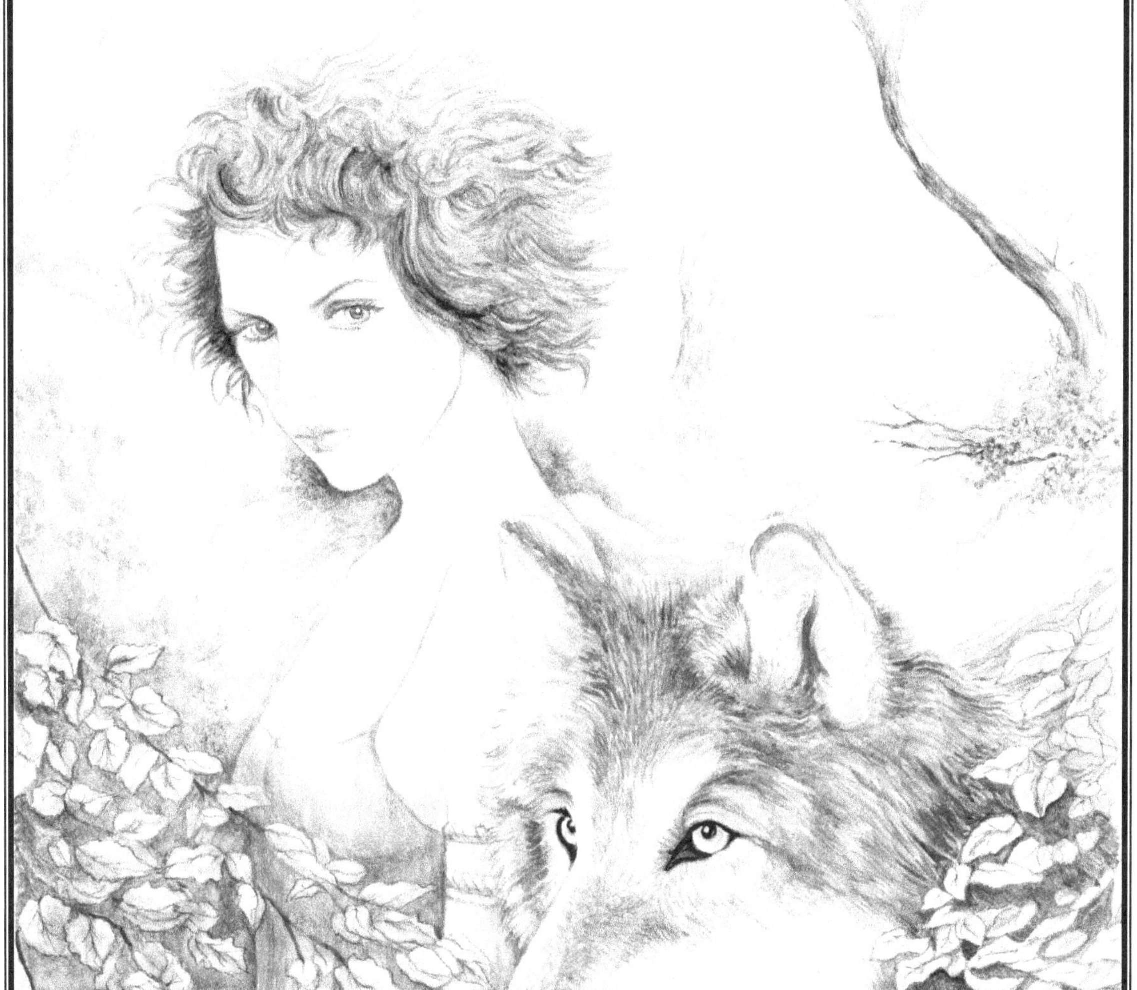

## Morgan Fitzsimons

# OLD COMPANIONS
## Morgan Fitzsimons Colour Magic Series

*In ancient days our ancestors revered the animals and birds as power animals and spirit guides. Some of Morgand paintings are in grescale so you can add colour, words and images on the reverse*

*The characters are unamed & open to your interpretation*

*Front Cover muse; Julie Carter, back Laura Daligan*
*Inside Julie, Laura, Hannah Titania, Karen Kay, Maggie Beth Sand, Jilly Paddock*

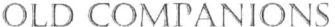

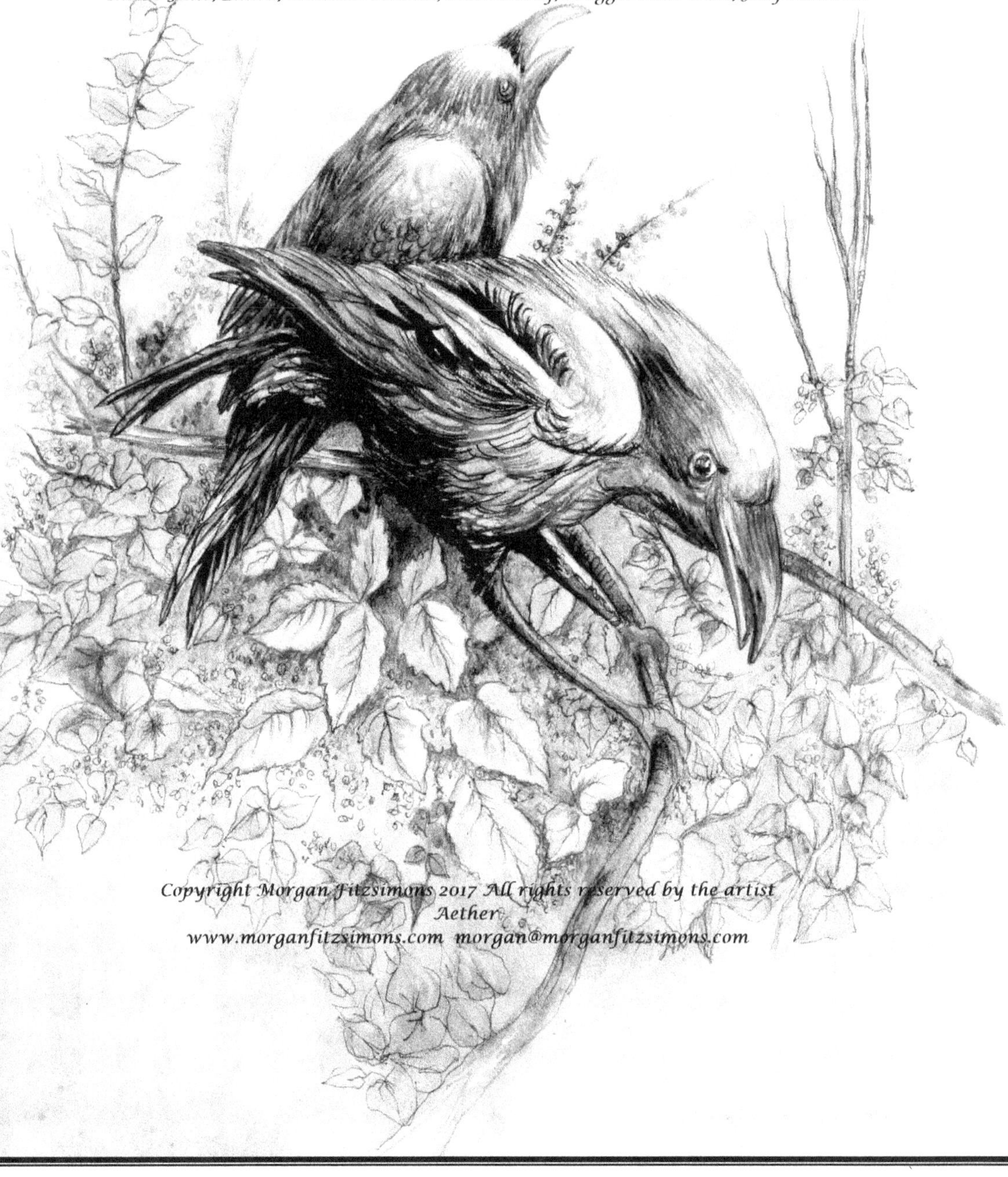

*Copyright Morgan Fitzsimons 2017 All rights reserved by the artist*
*Aether*
*www.morganfitzsimons.com  morgan@morganfitzsimons.com*

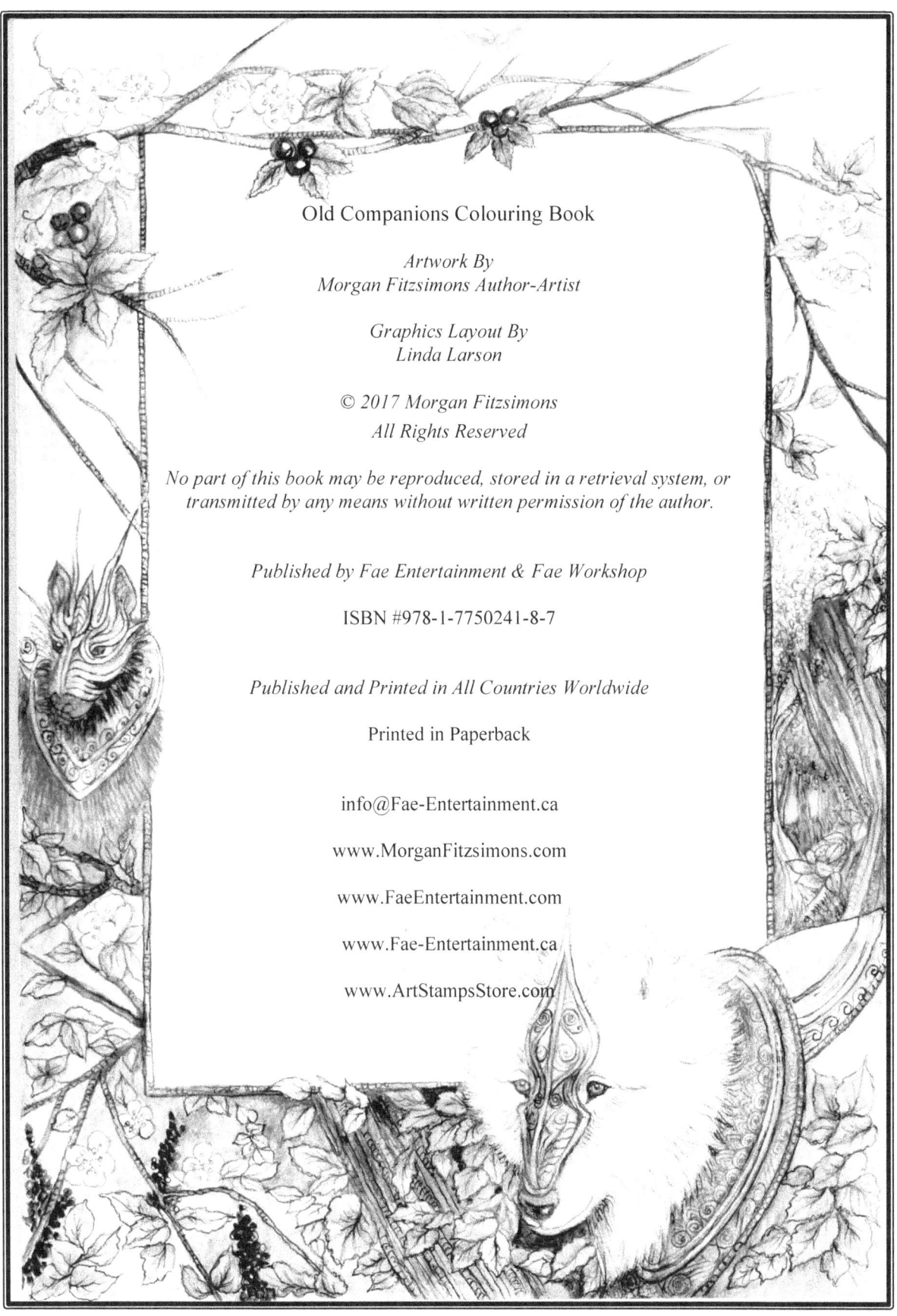

Old Companions Colouring Book

*Artwork By*
*Morgan Fitzsimons Author-Artist*

*Graphics Layout By*
*Linda Larson*

© 2017 Morgan Fitzsimons
*All Rights Reserved*

*No part of this book may be reproduced, stored in a retrieval system, or transmitted by any means without written permission of the author.*

*Published by Fae Entertainment & Fae Workshop*

ISBN #978-1-7750241-8-7

*Published and Printed in All Countries Worldwide*

Printed in Paperback

info@Fae-Entertainment.ca

www.MorganFitzsimons.com

www.FaeEntertainment.com

www.Fae-Entertainment.ca

www.ArtStampsStore.com

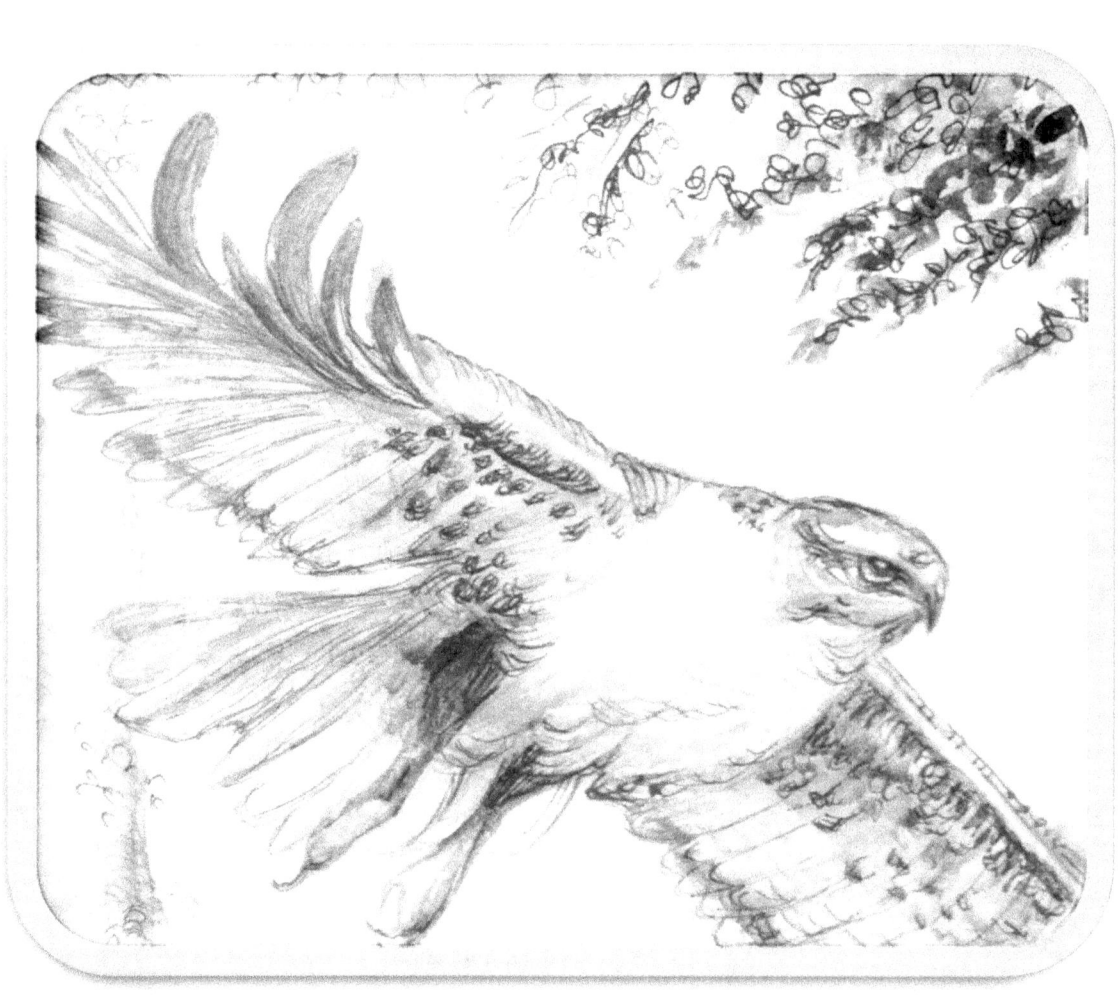

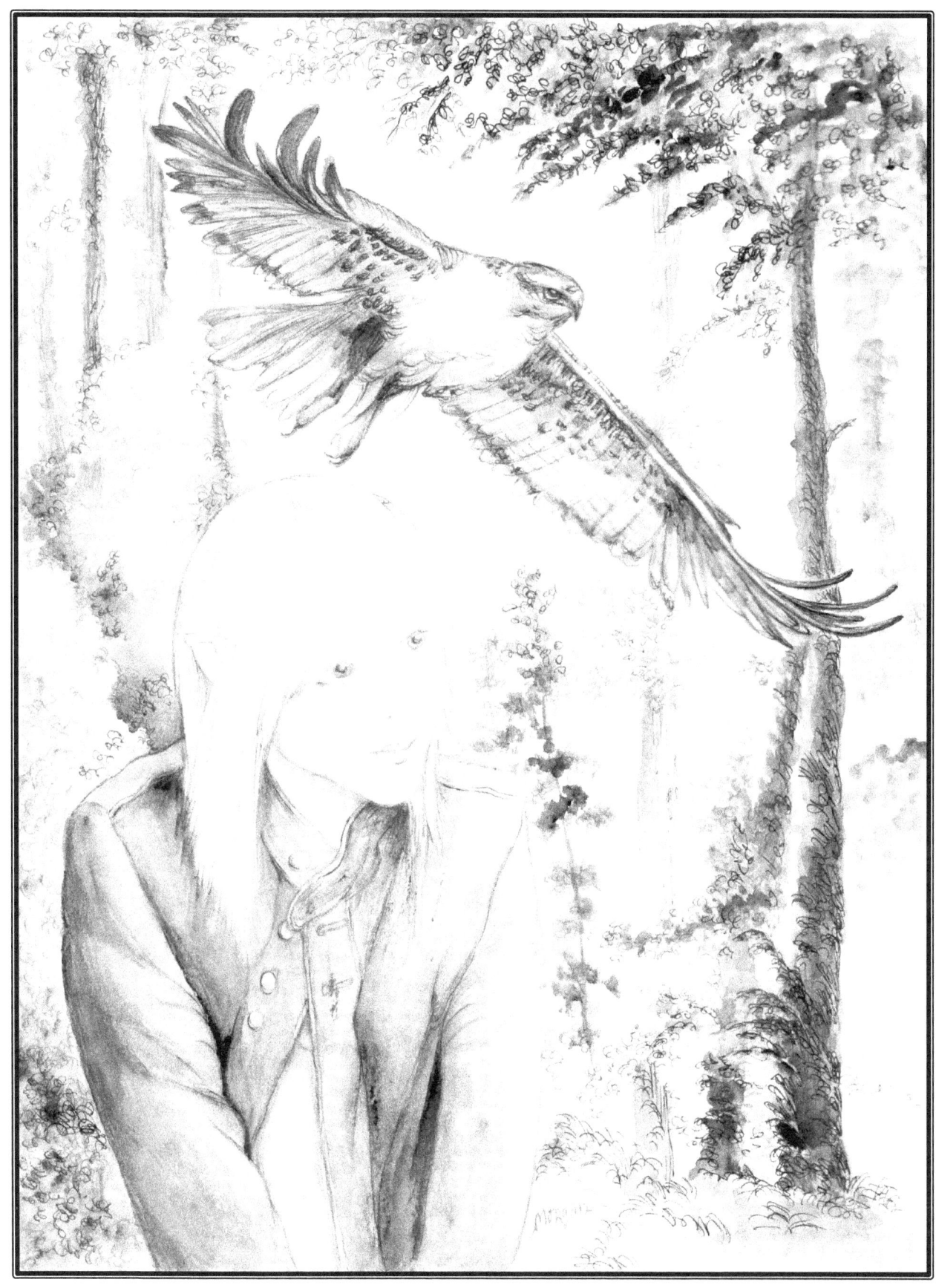

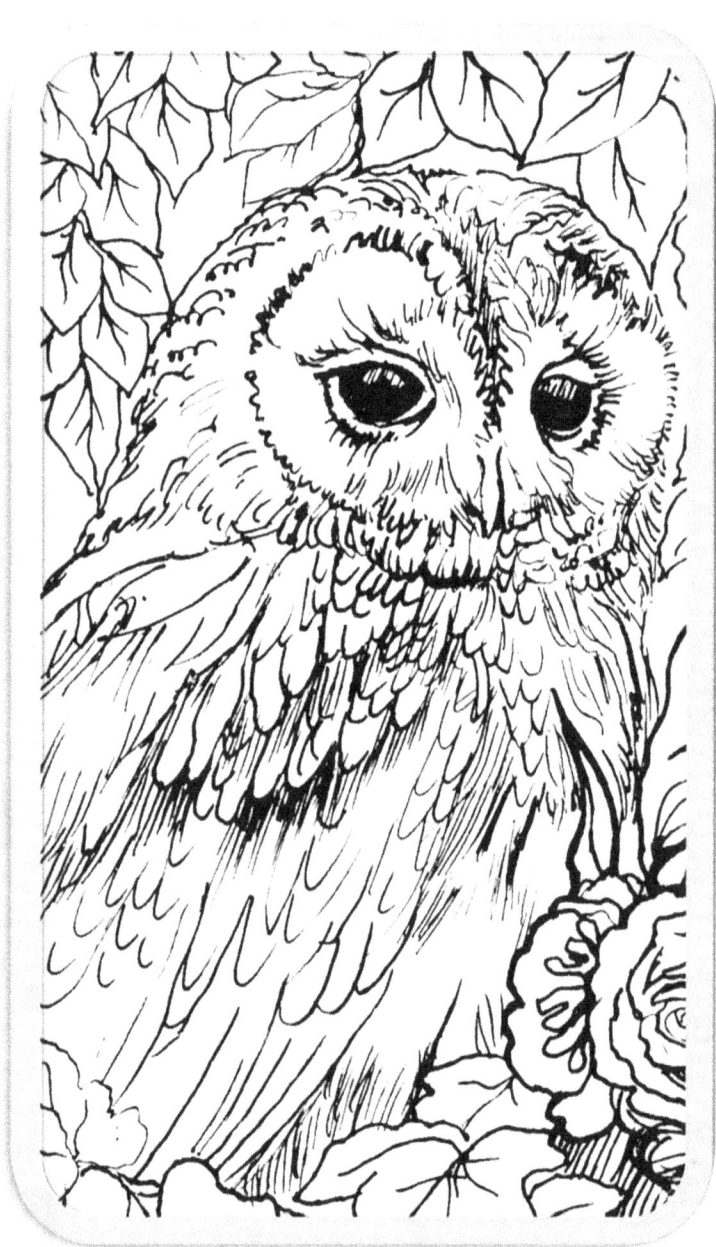

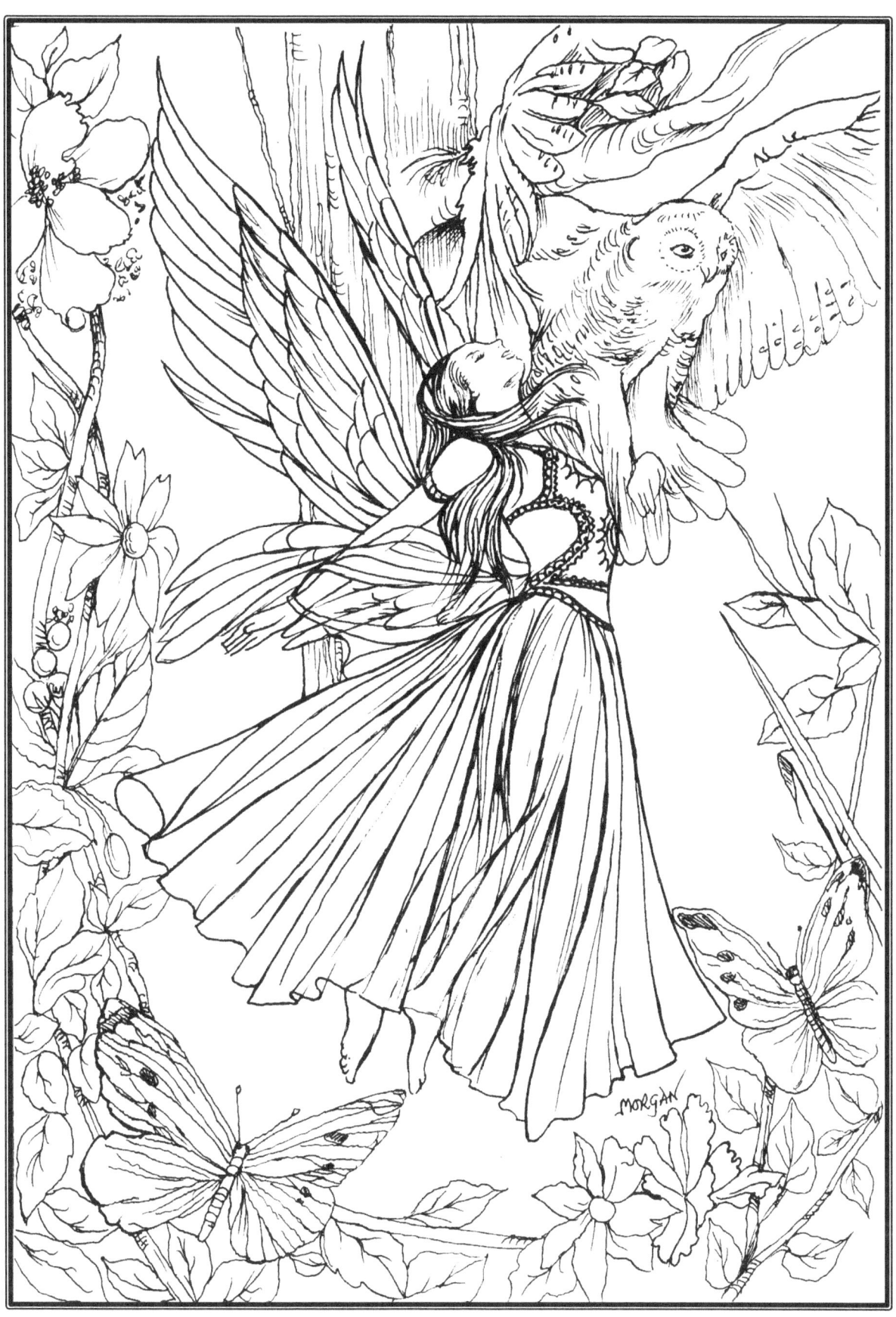

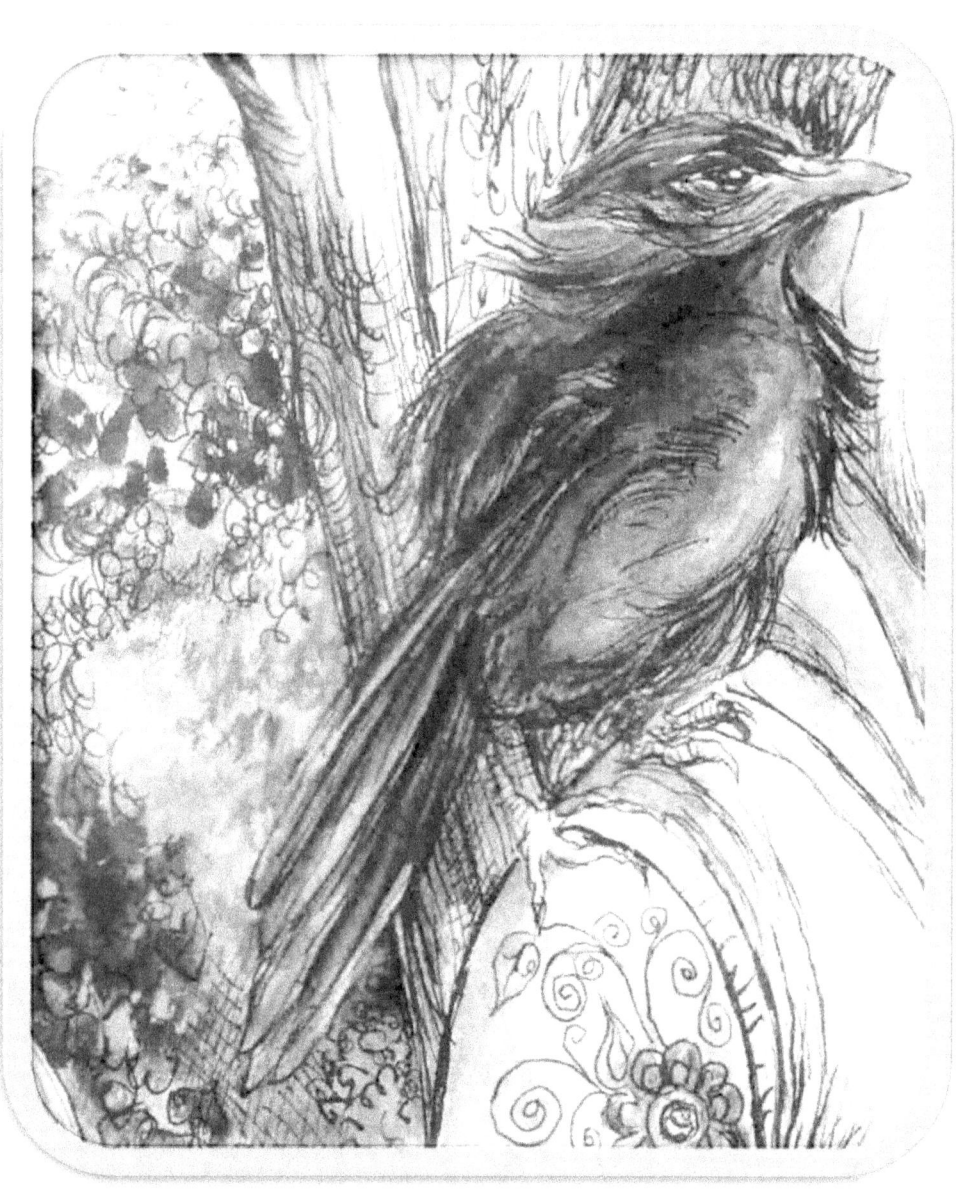

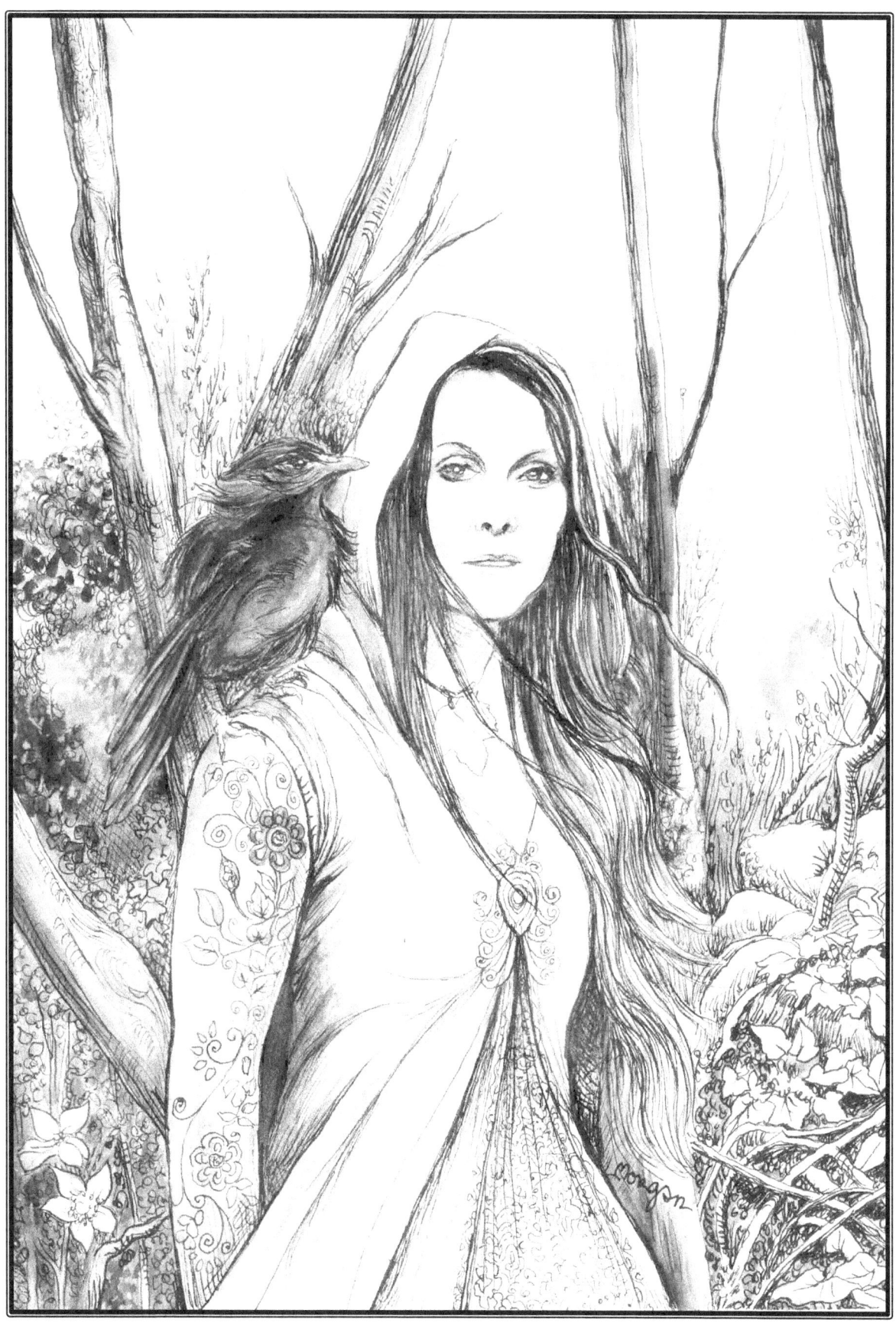

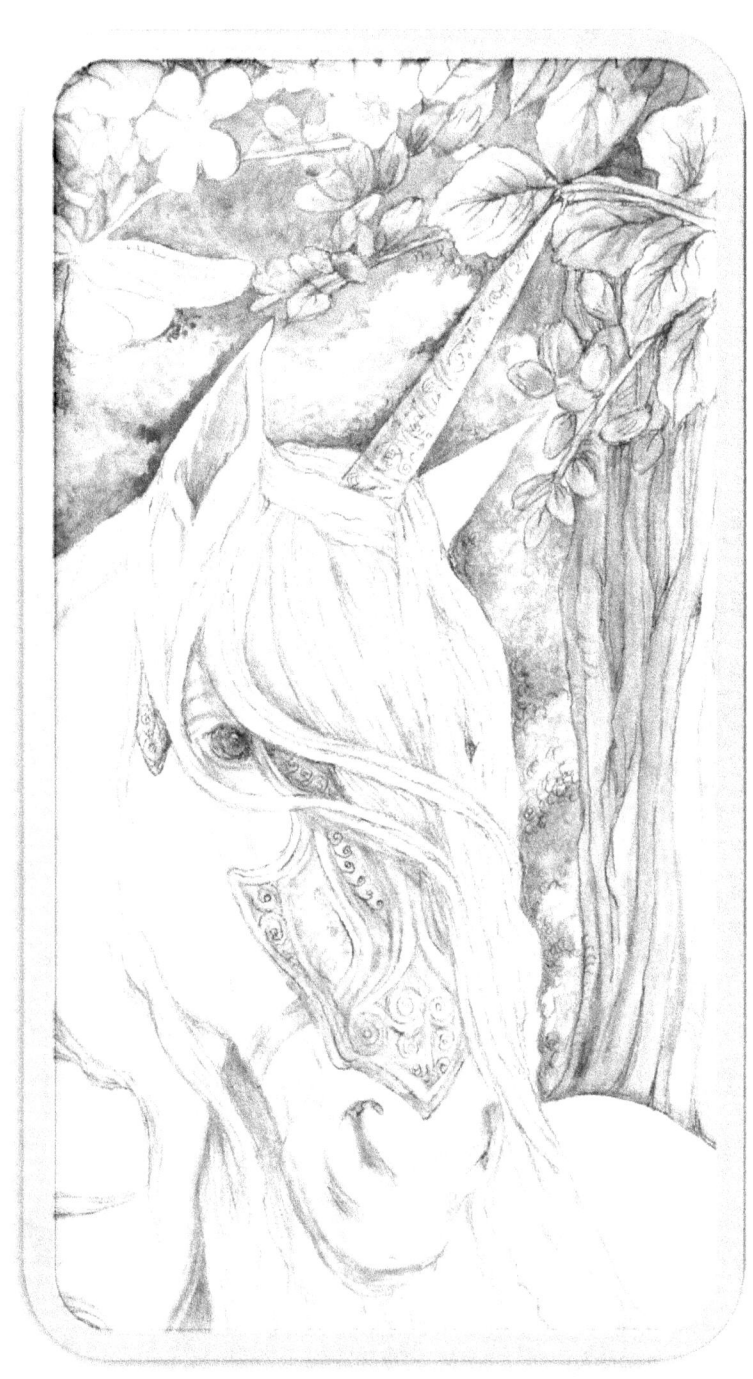

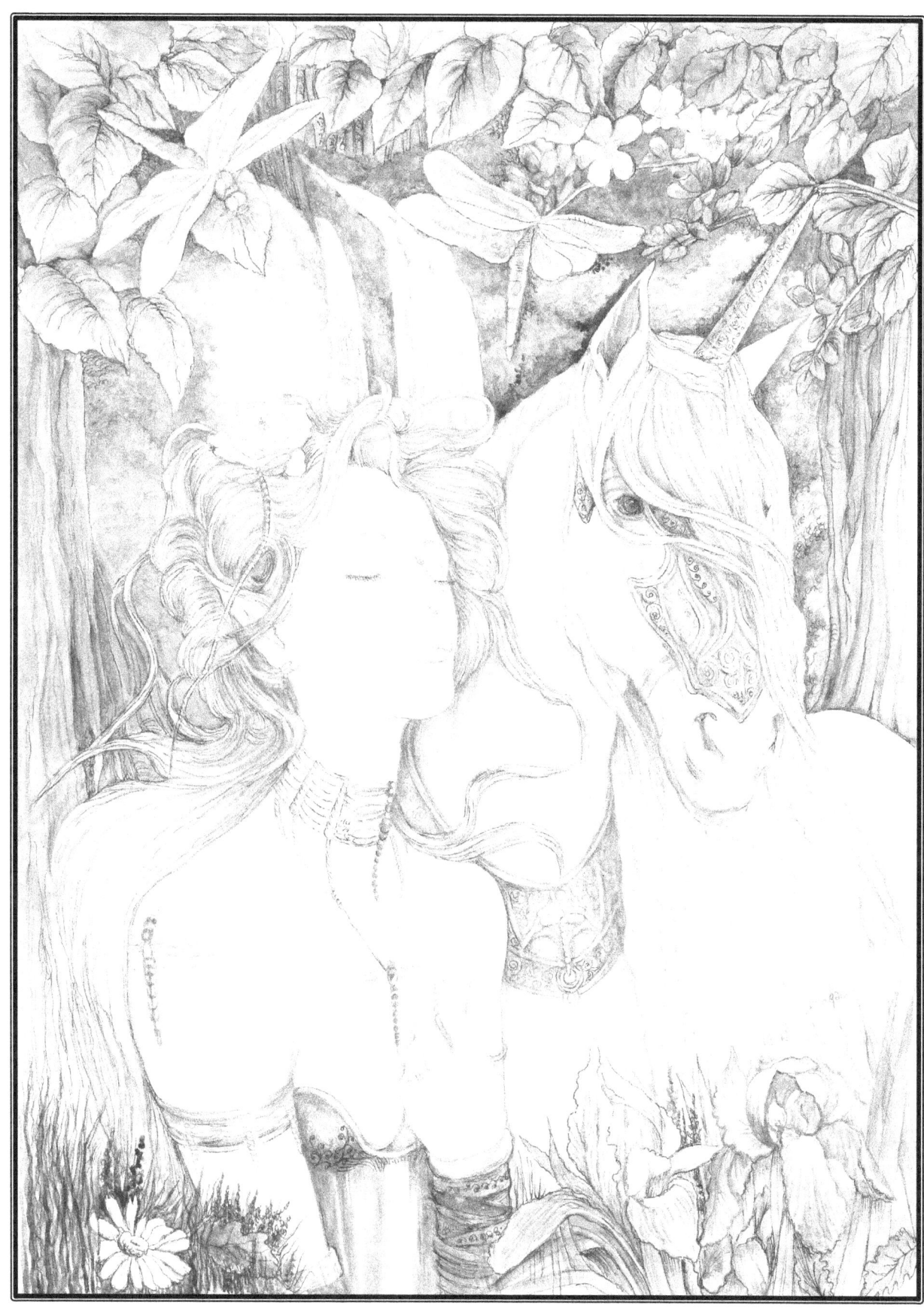

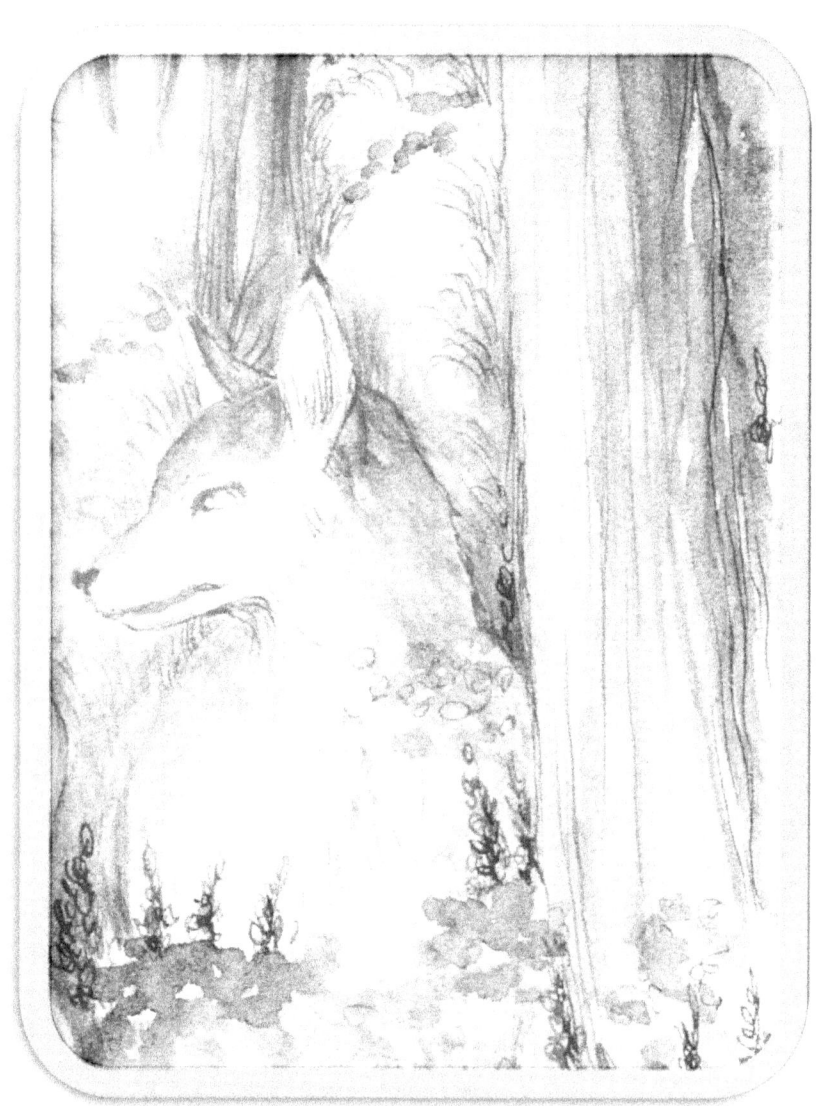

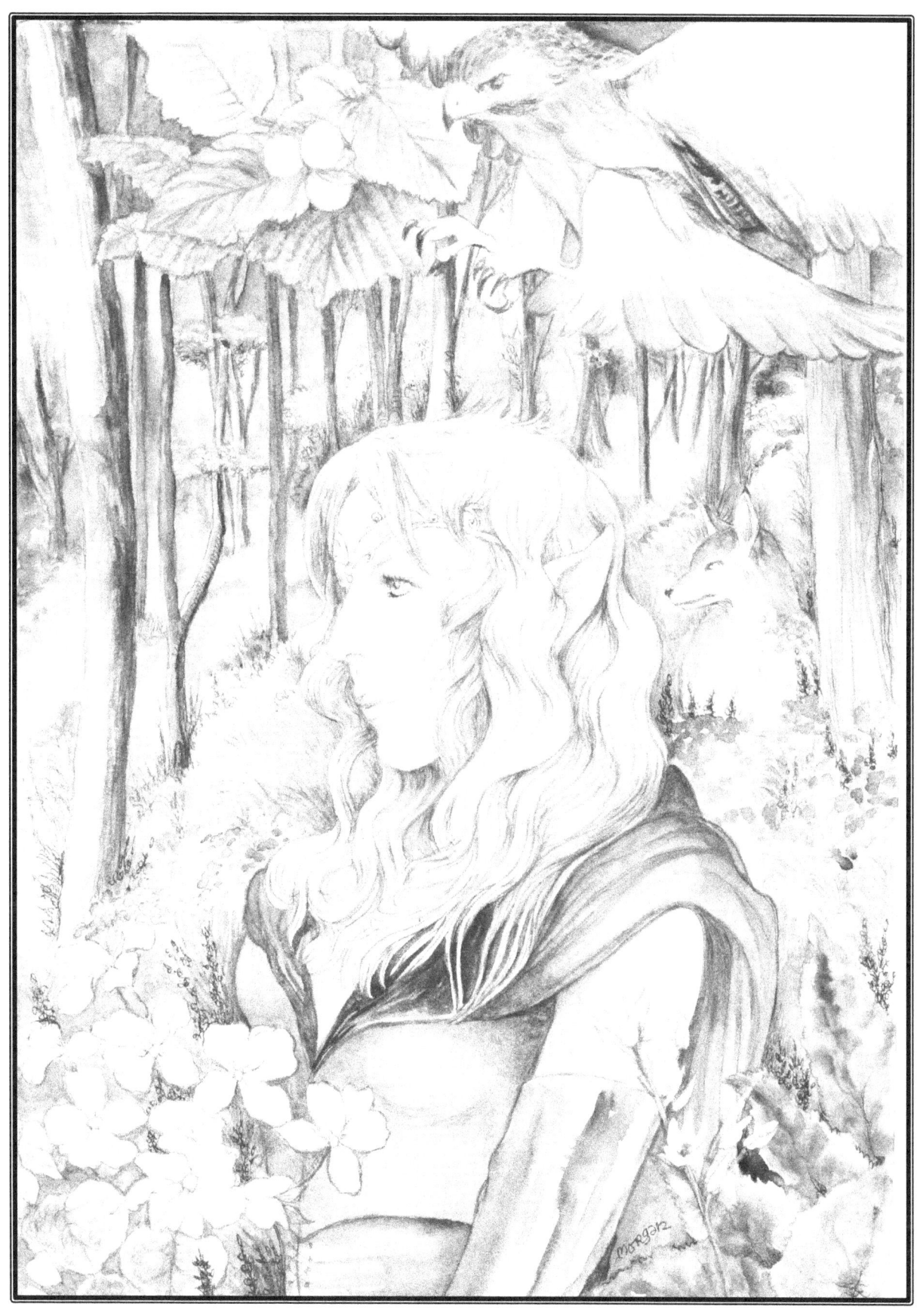

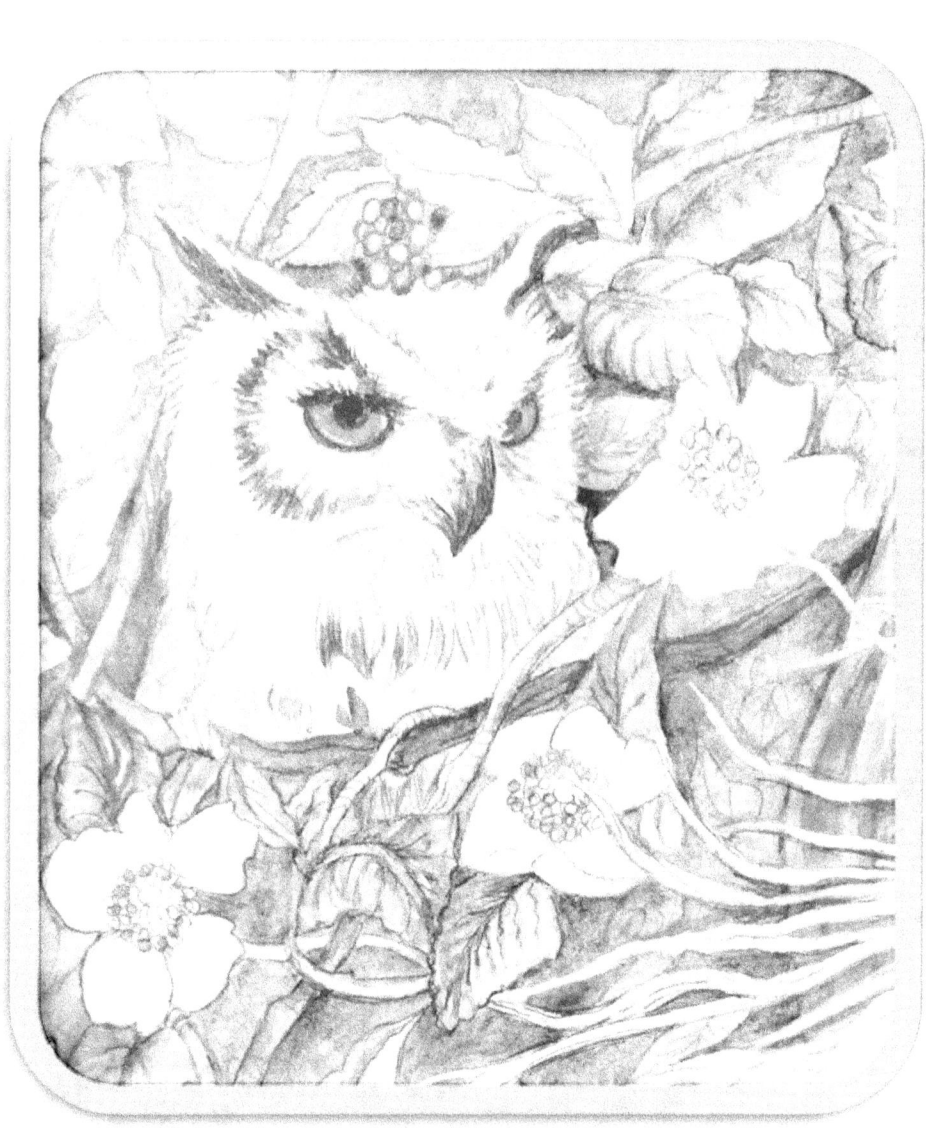

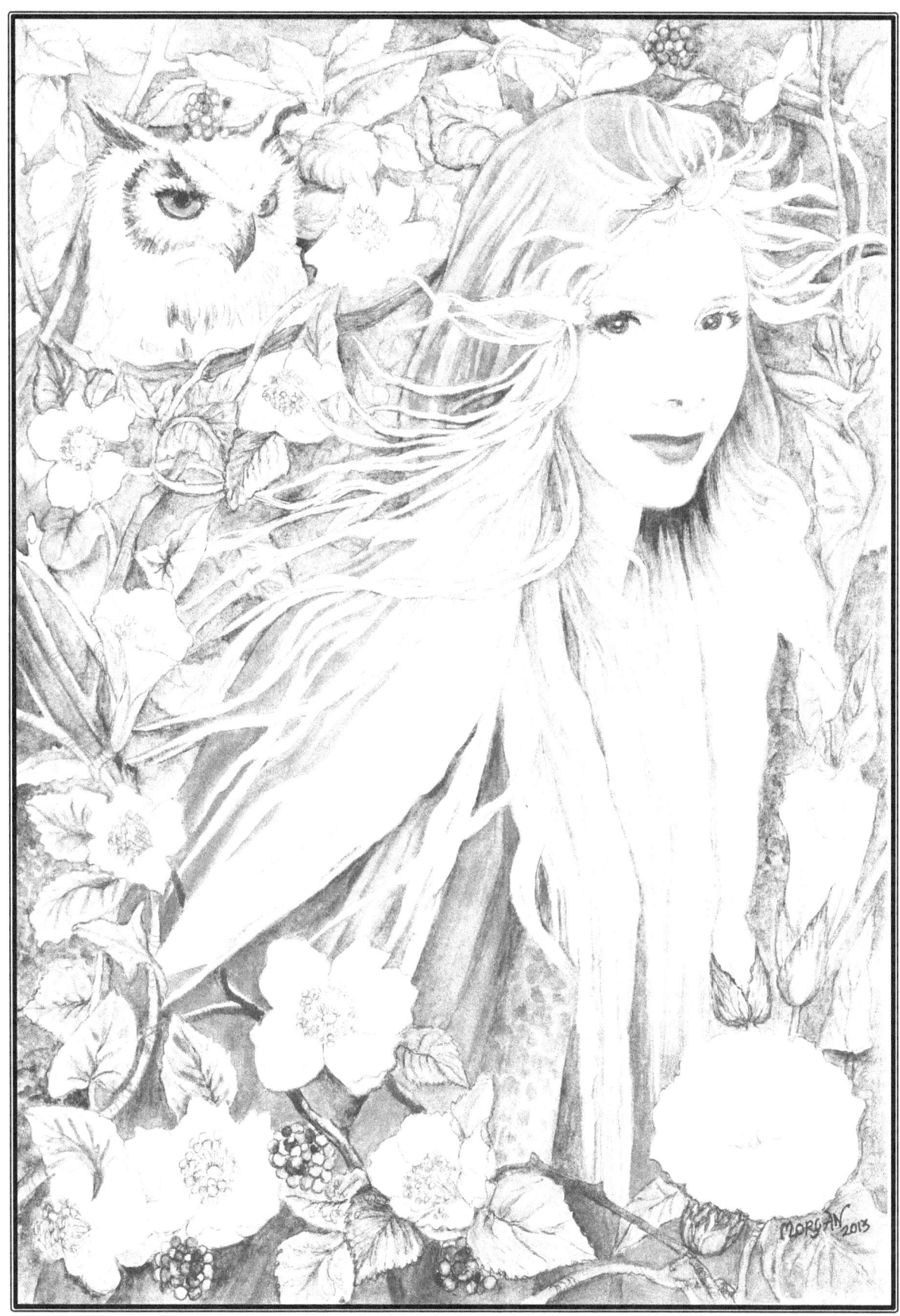

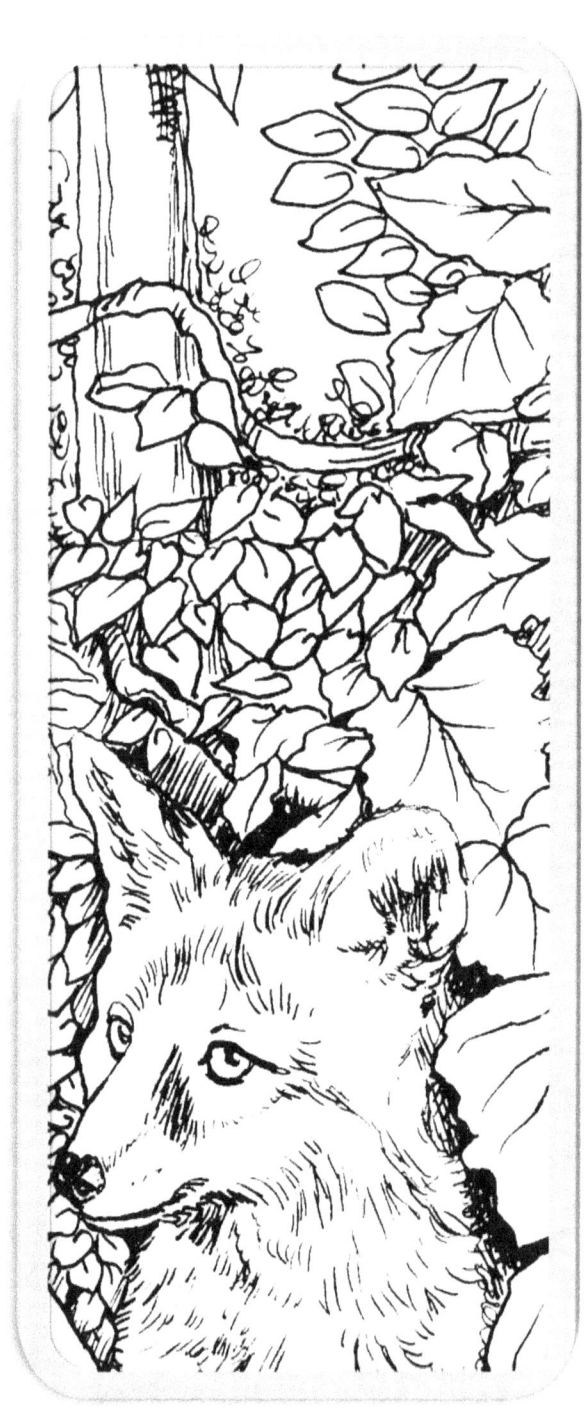

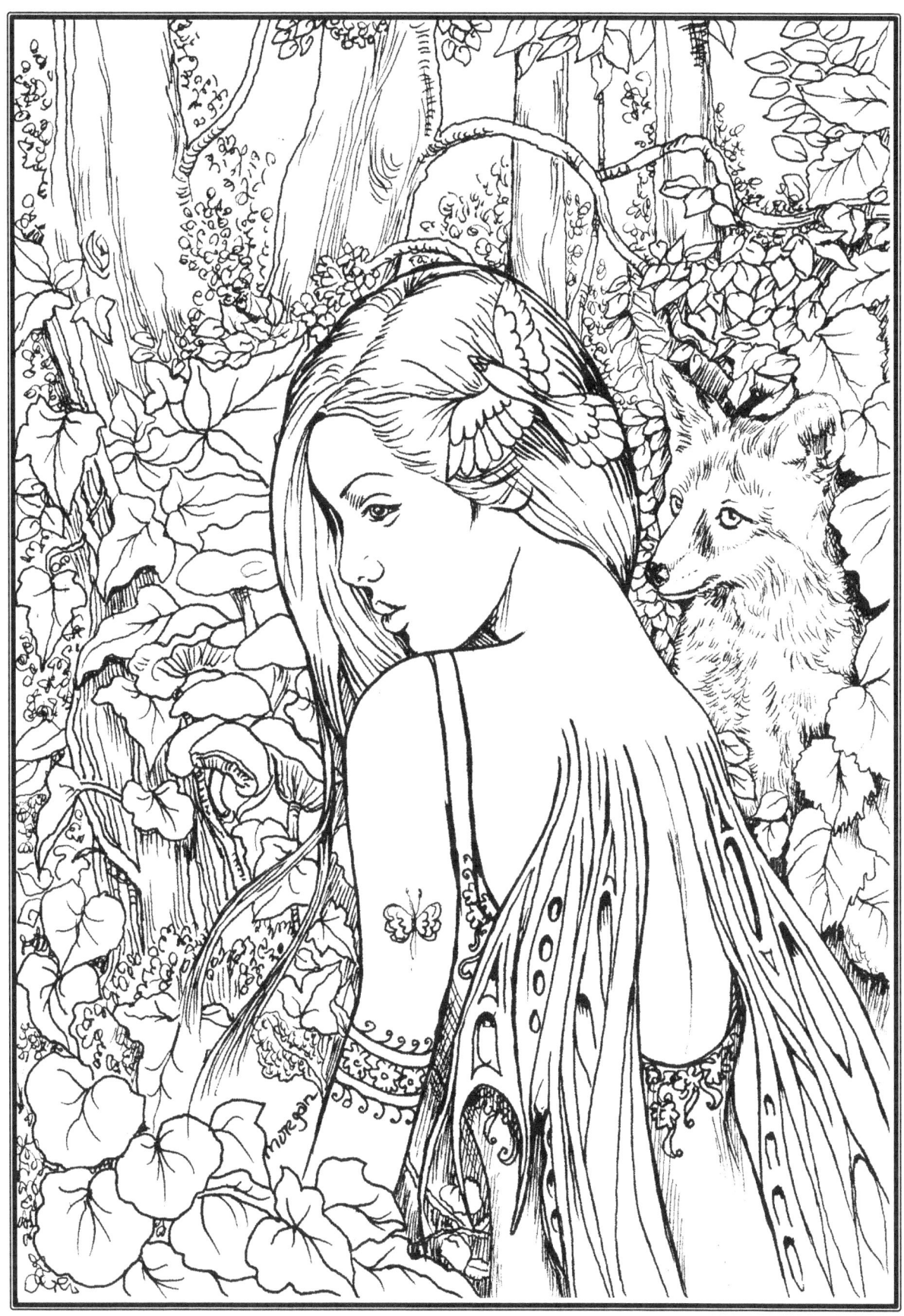

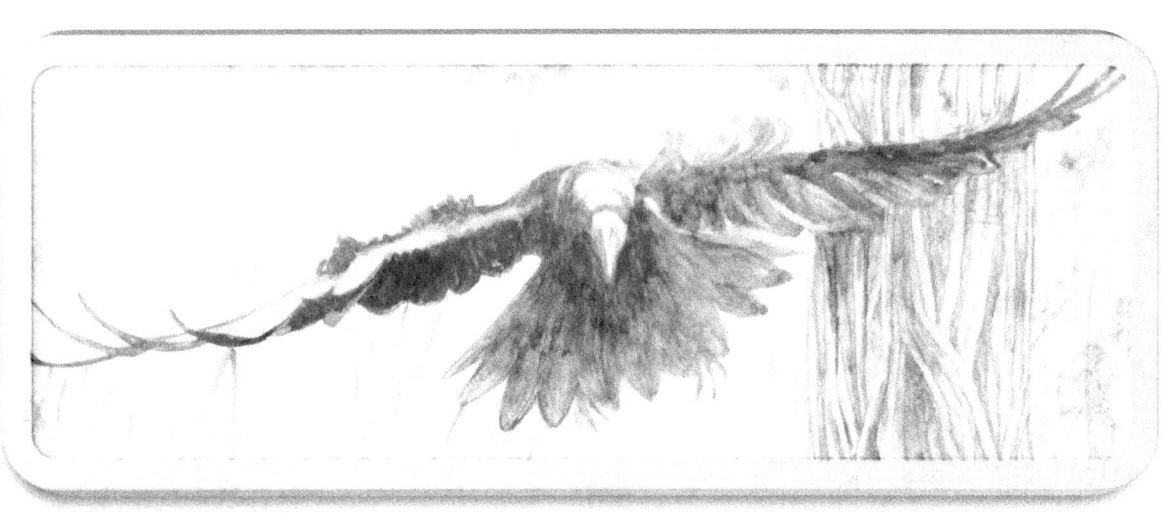

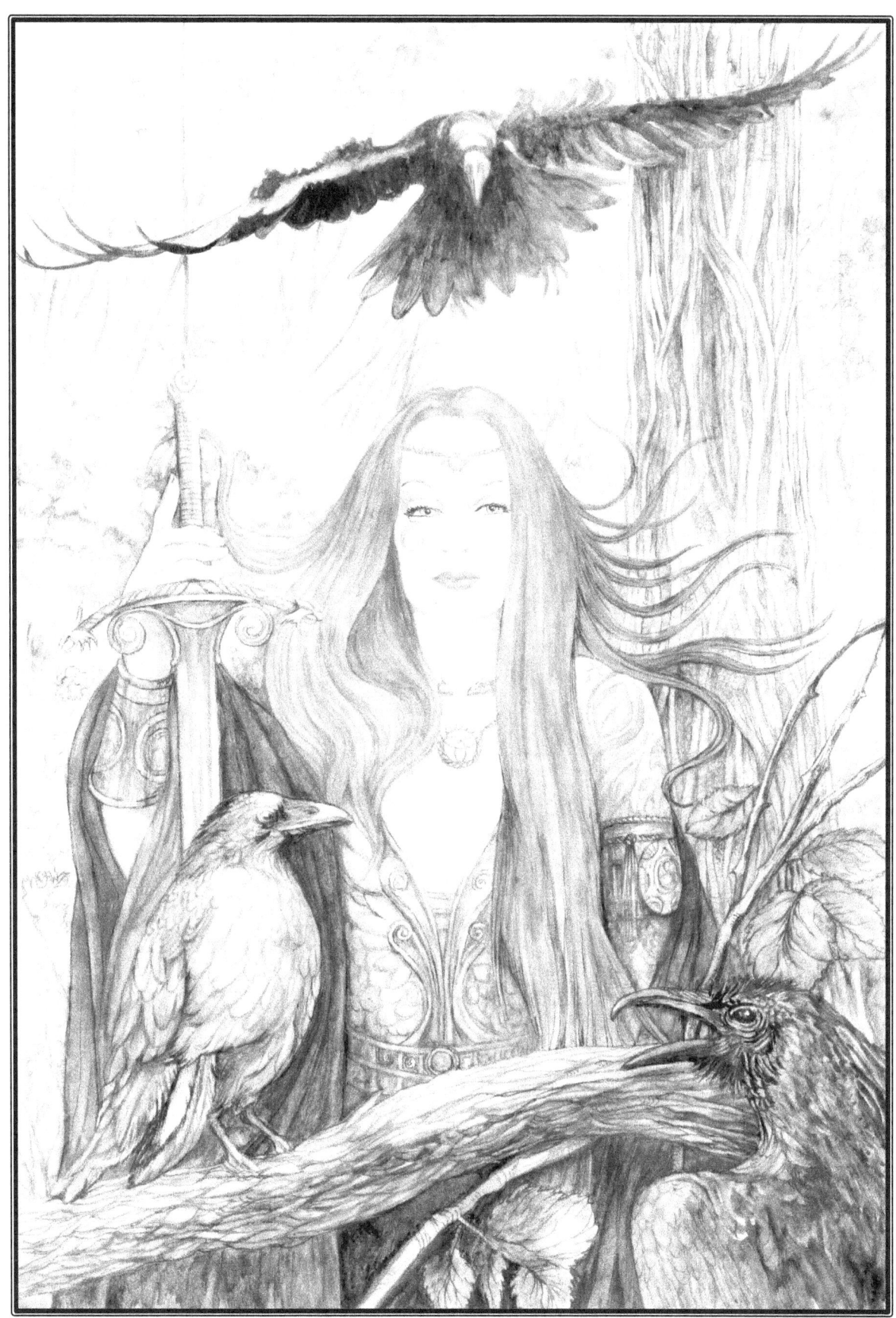

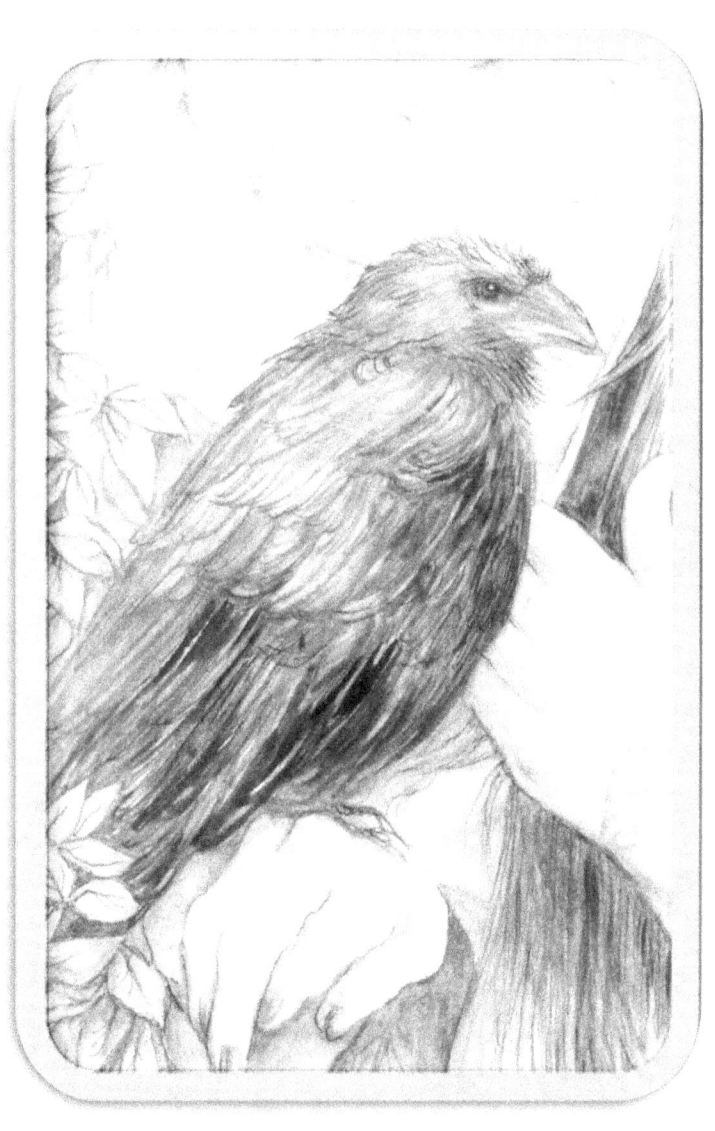

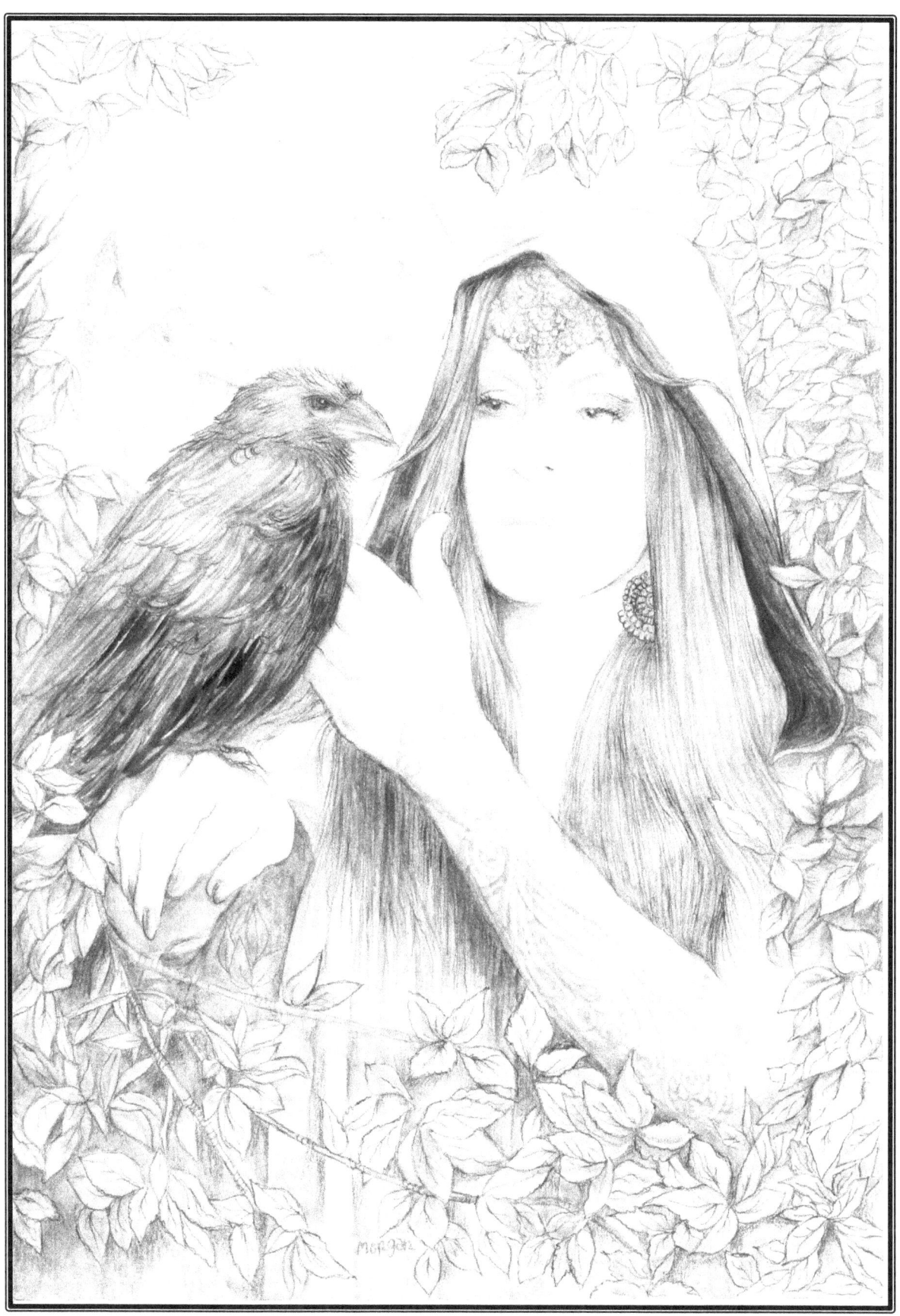

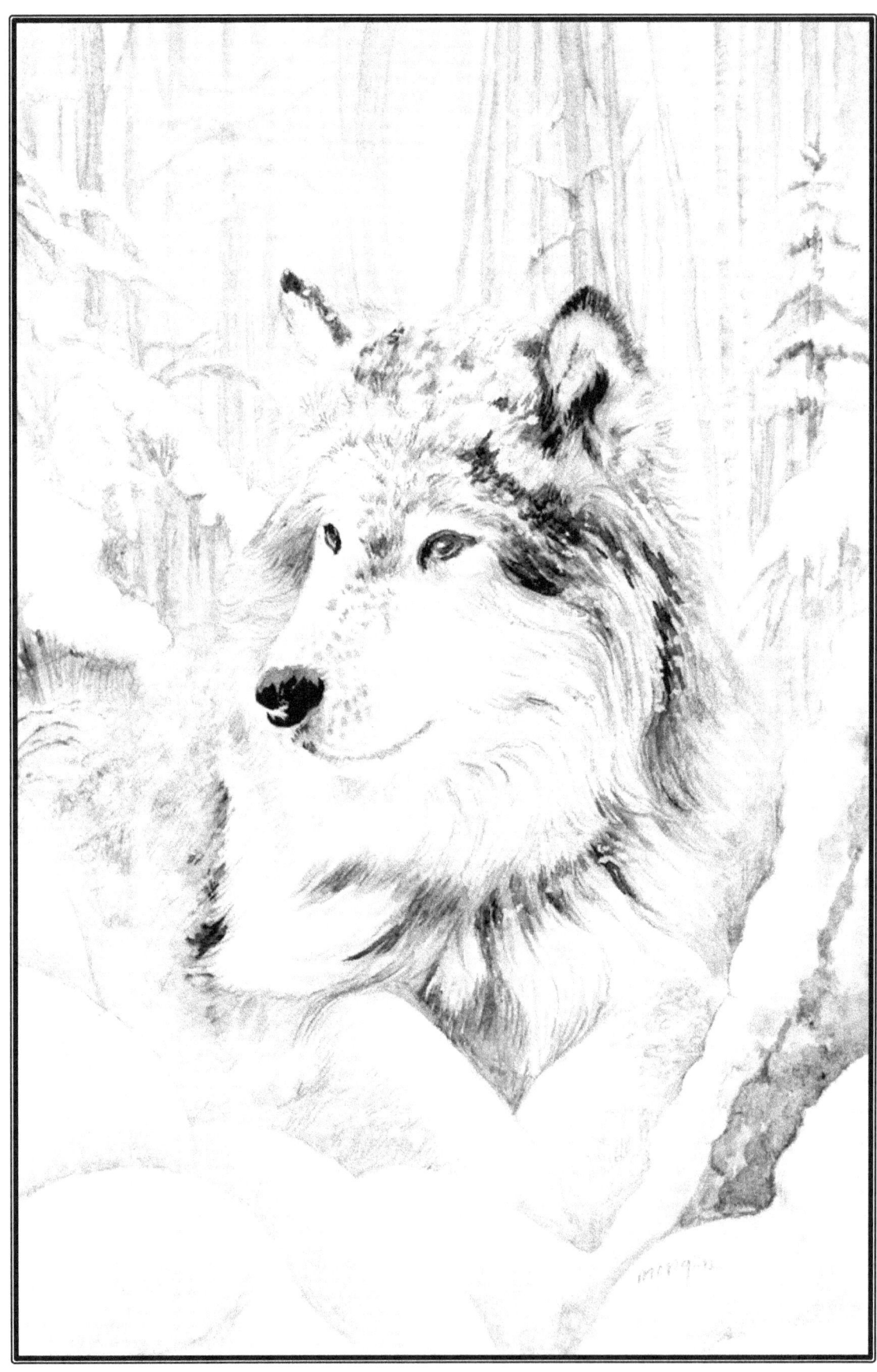

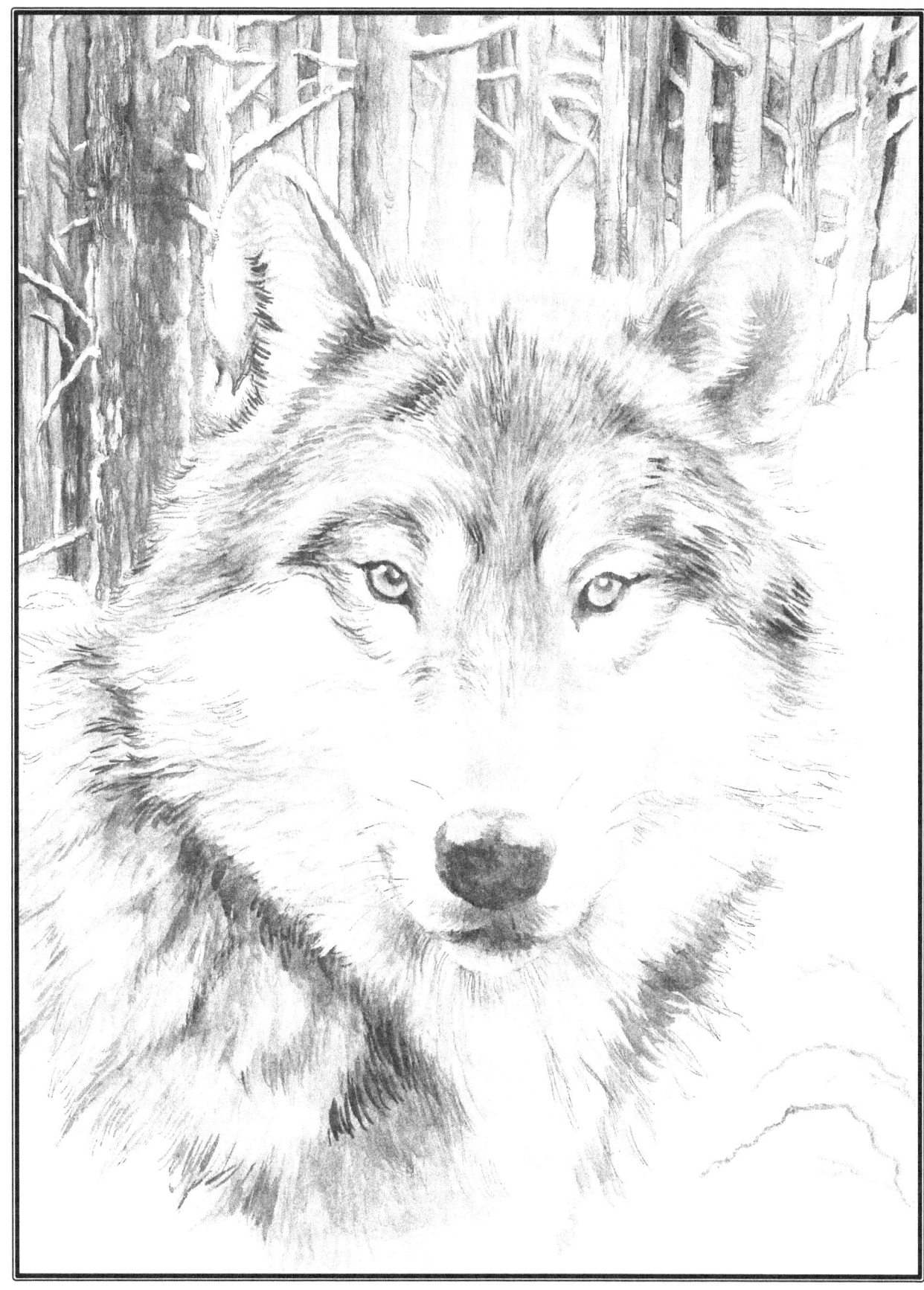

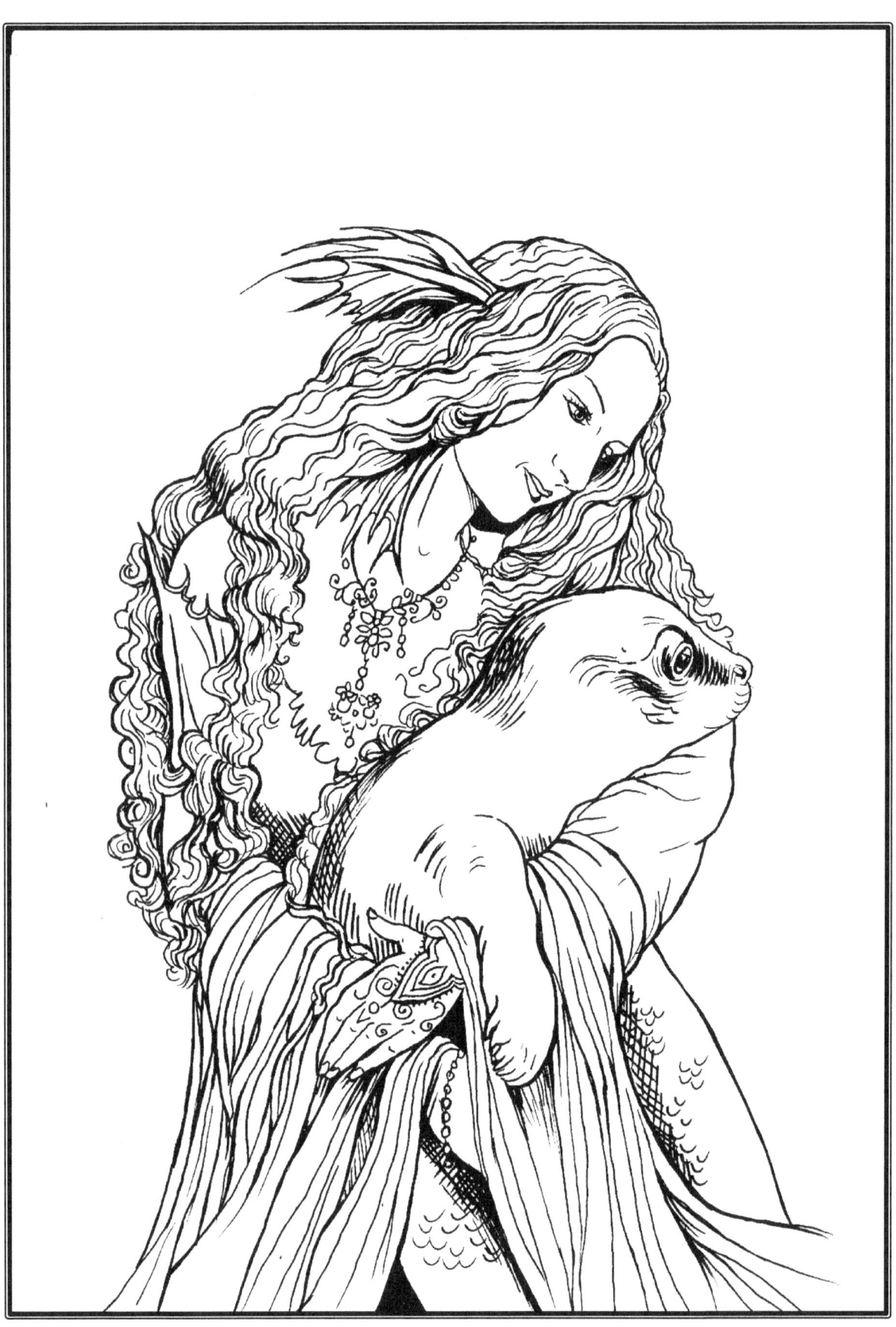

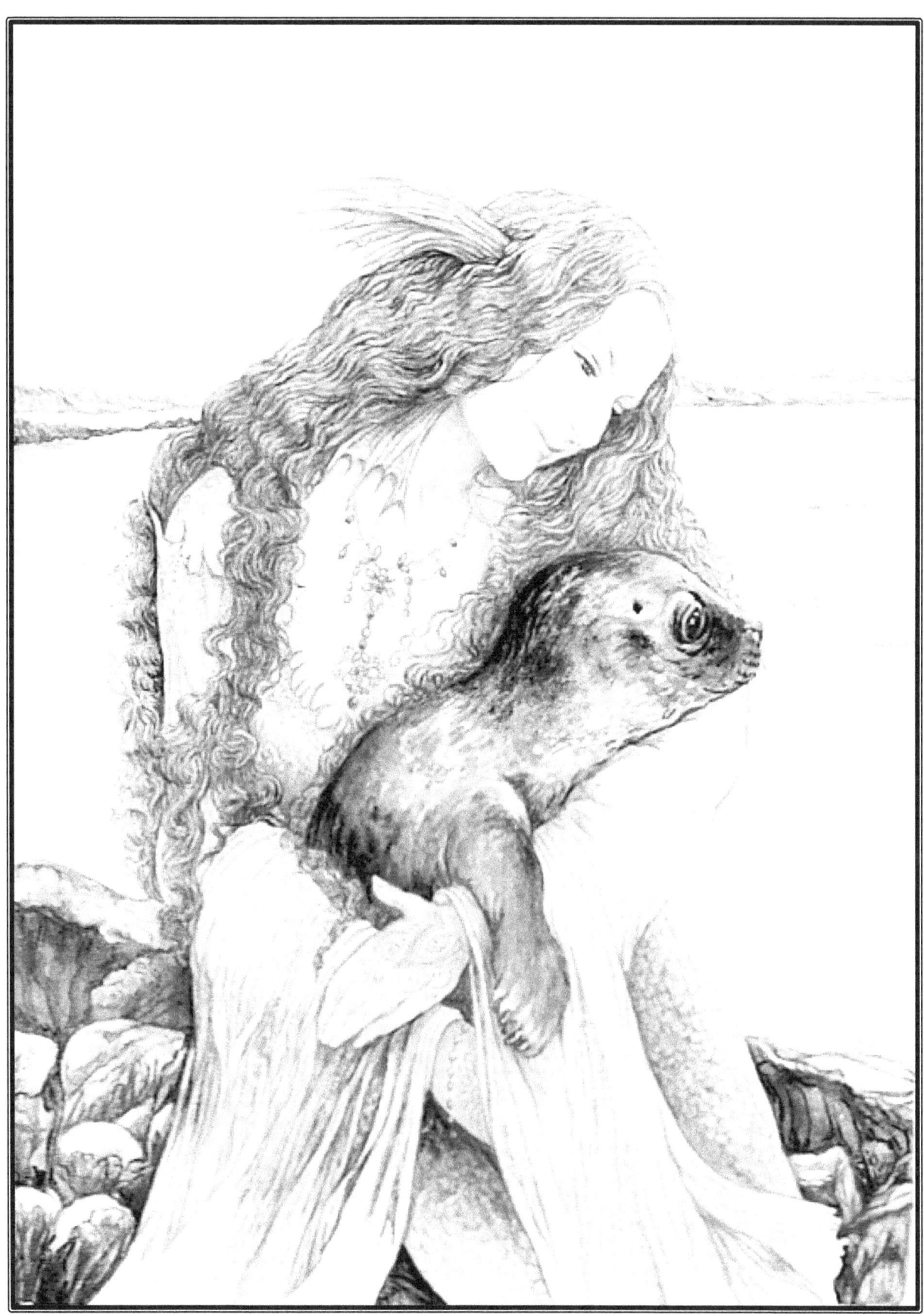

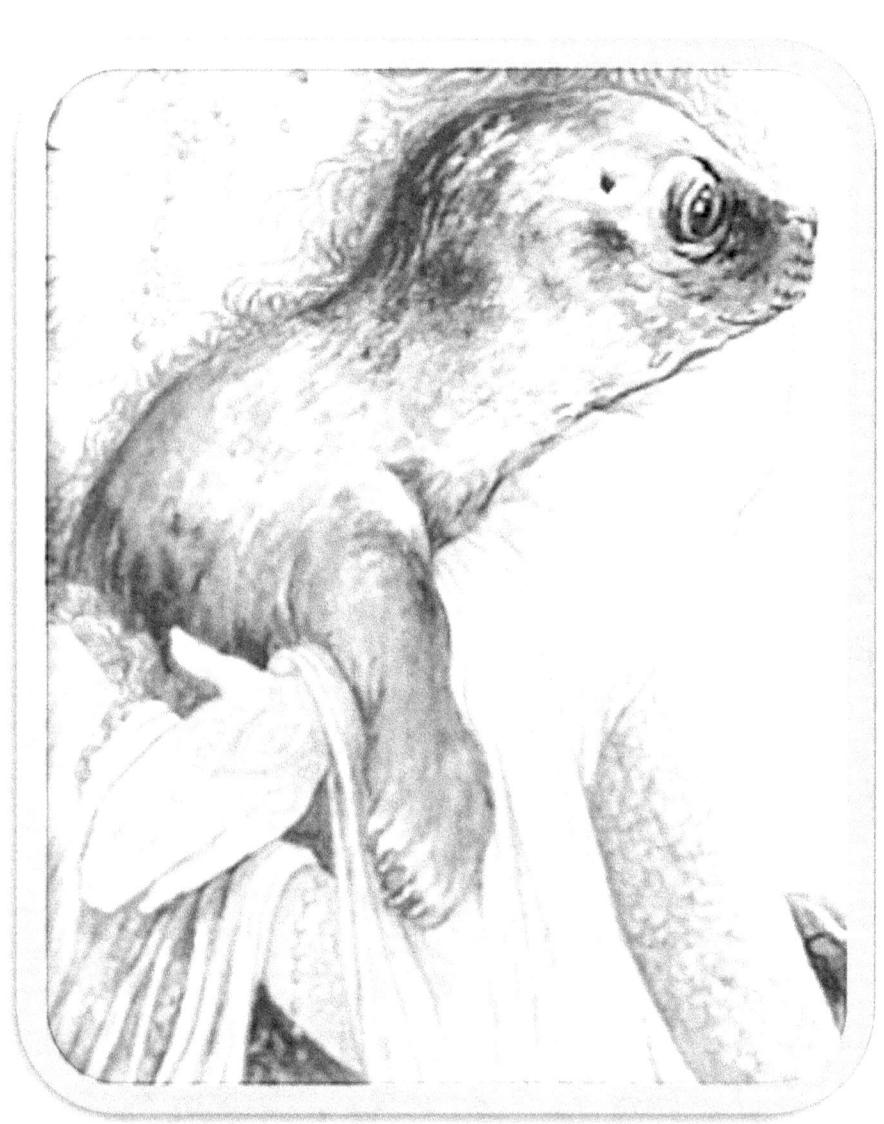

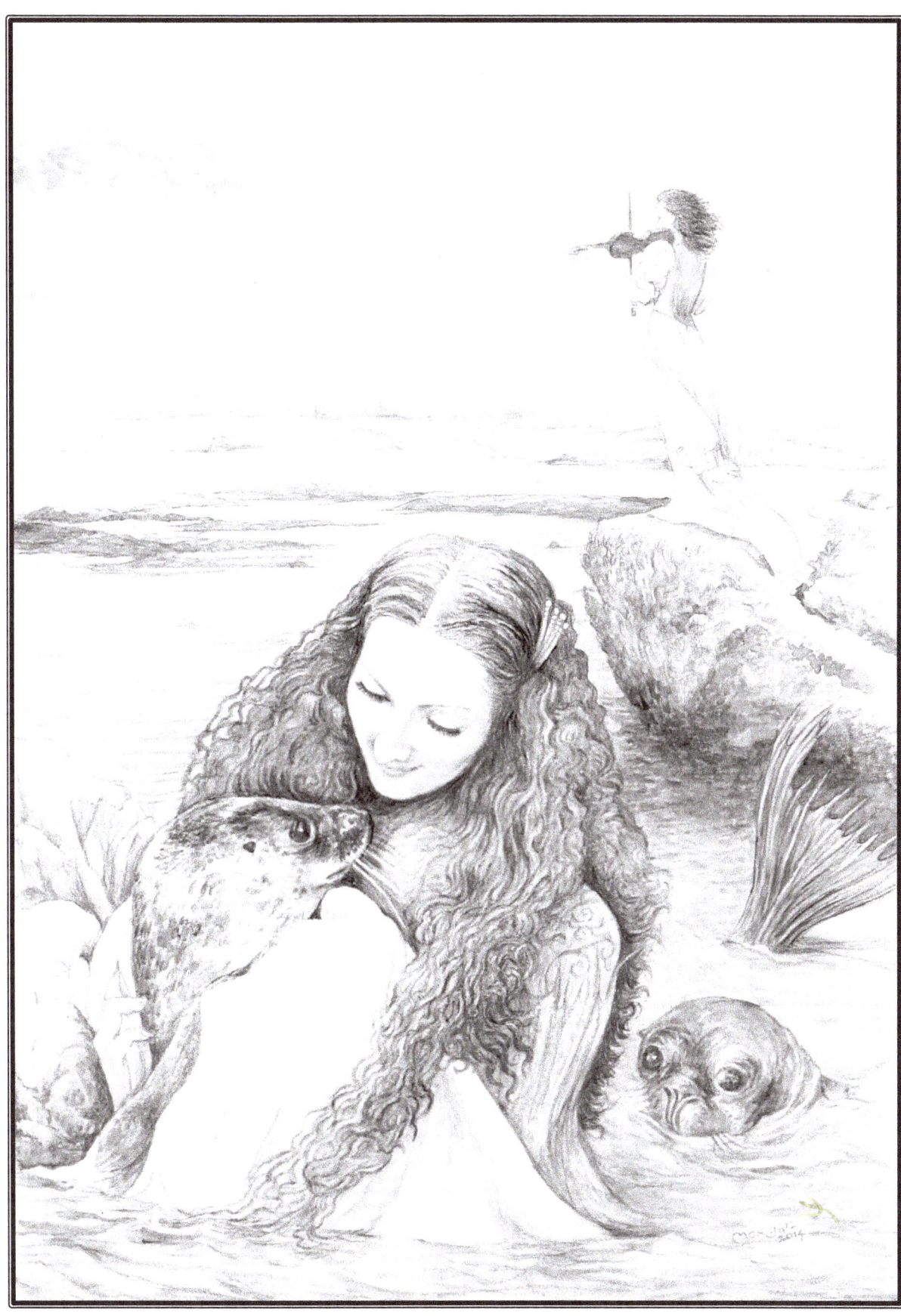

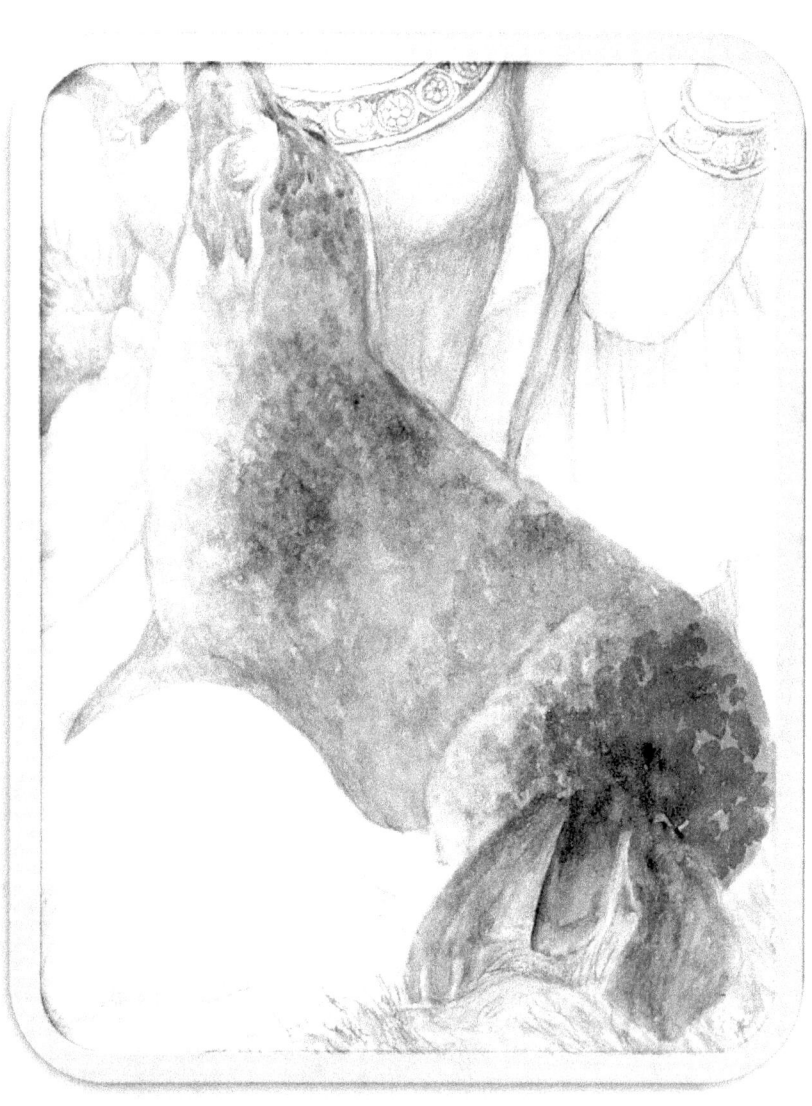

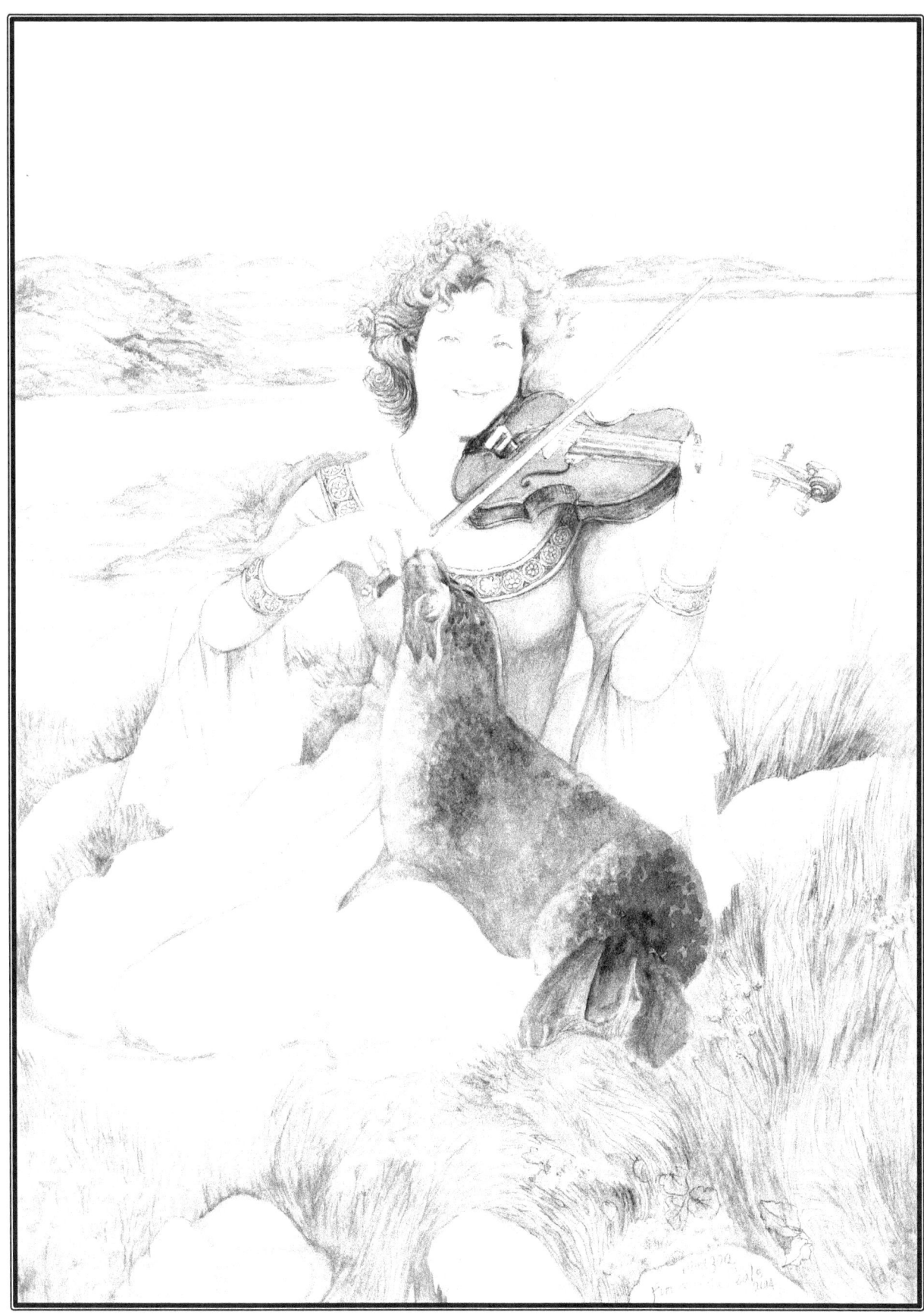

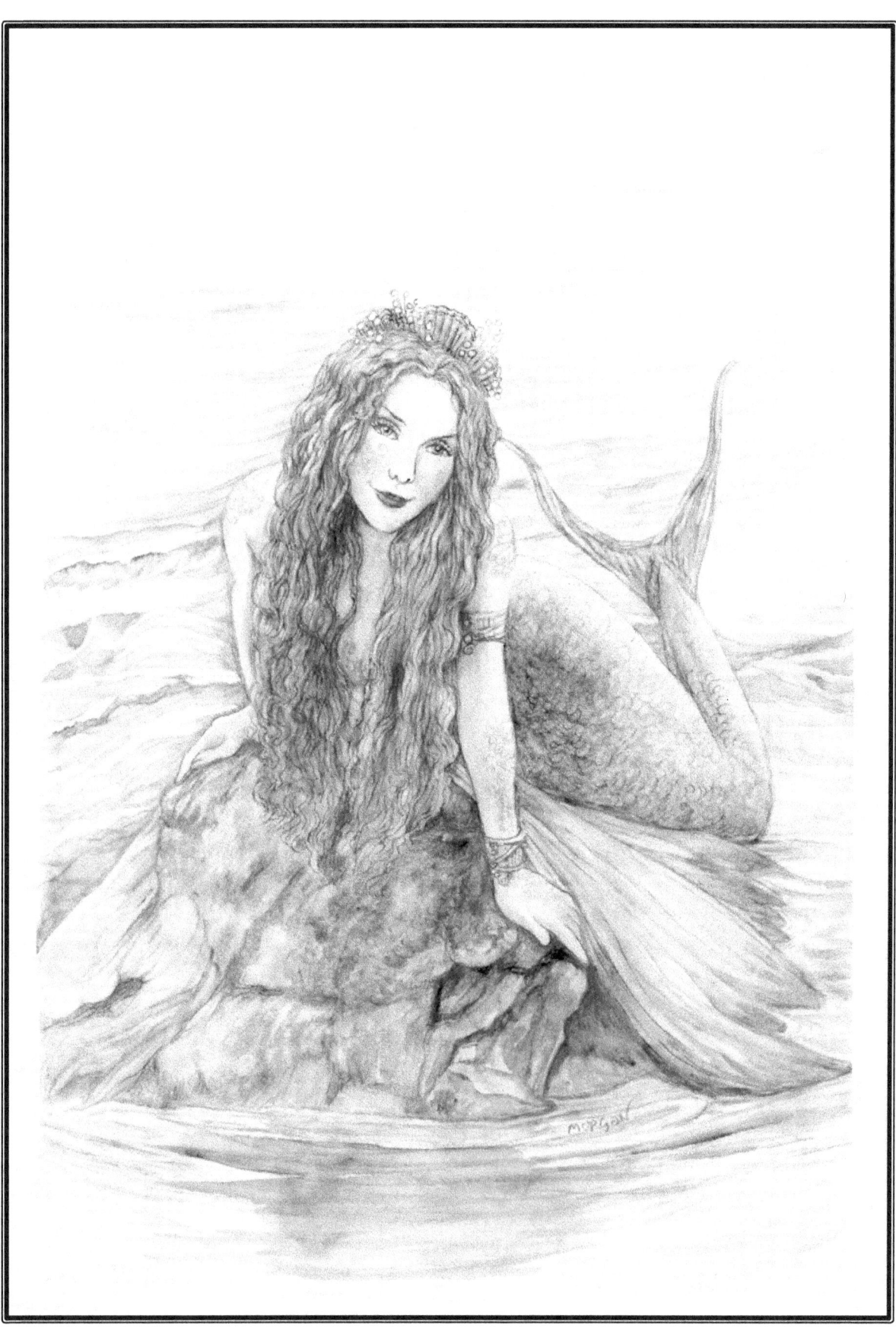

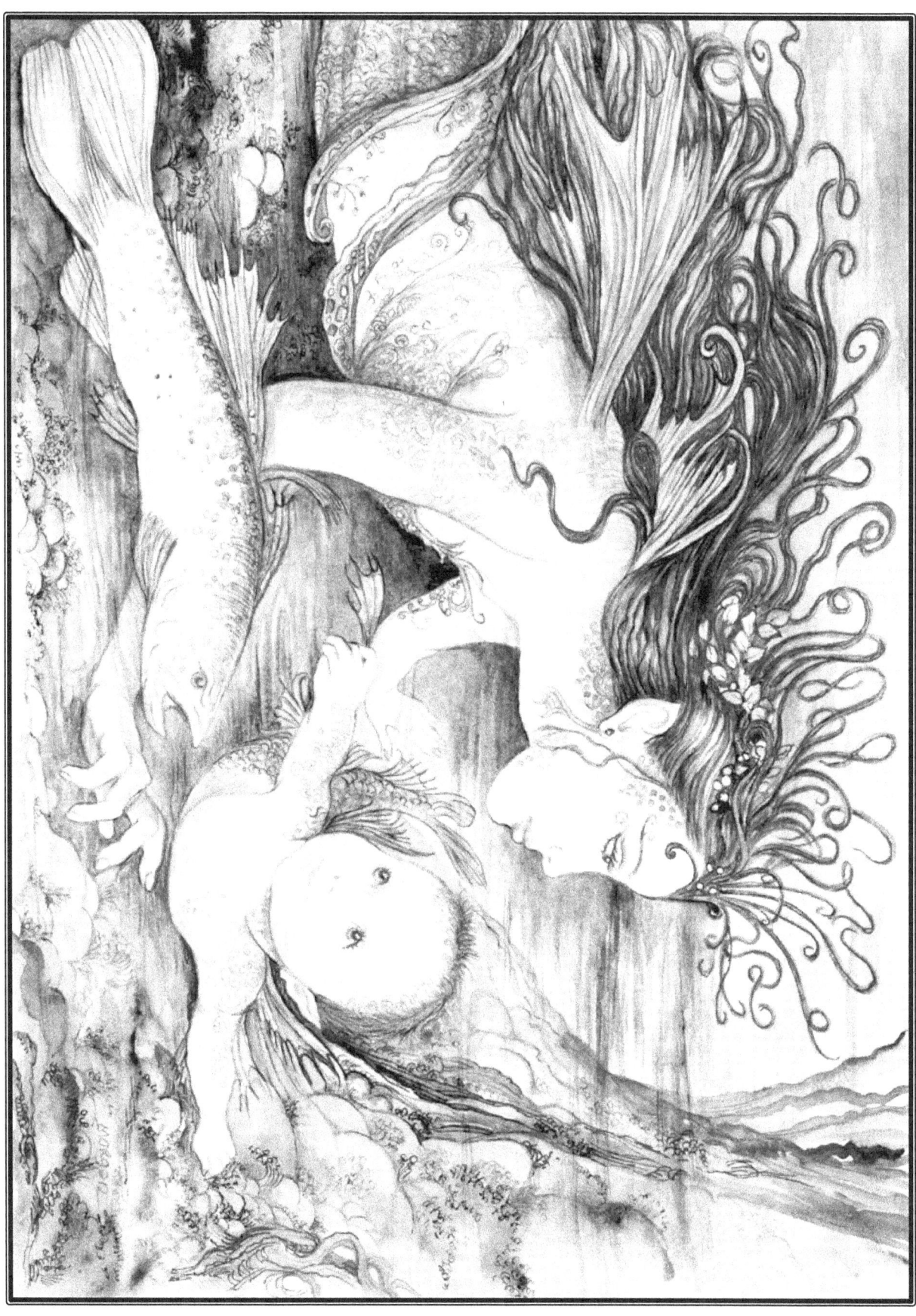

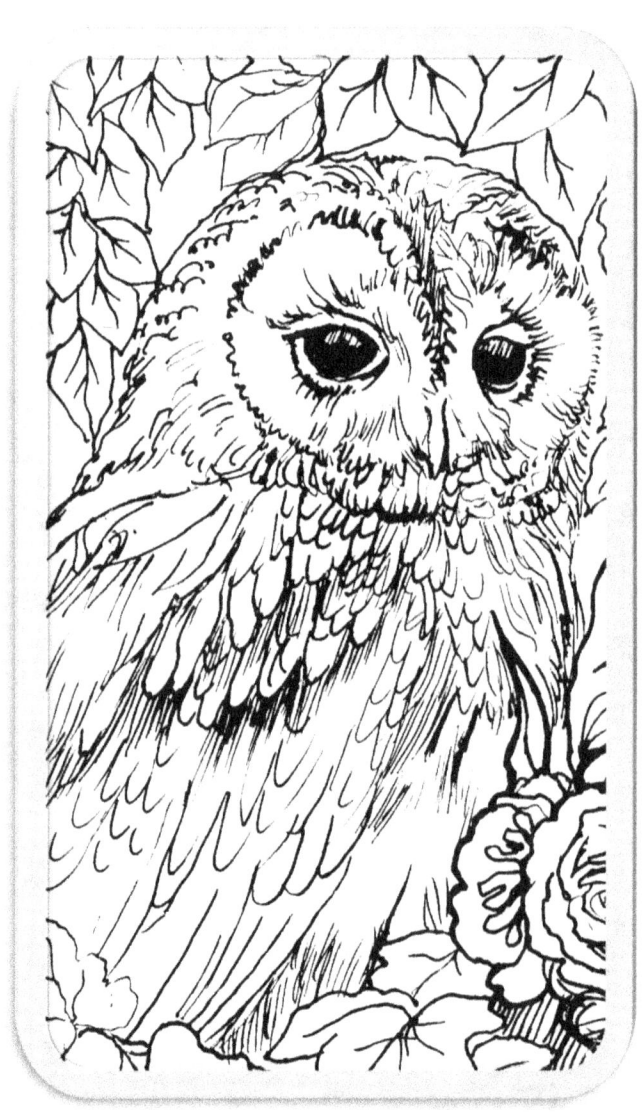

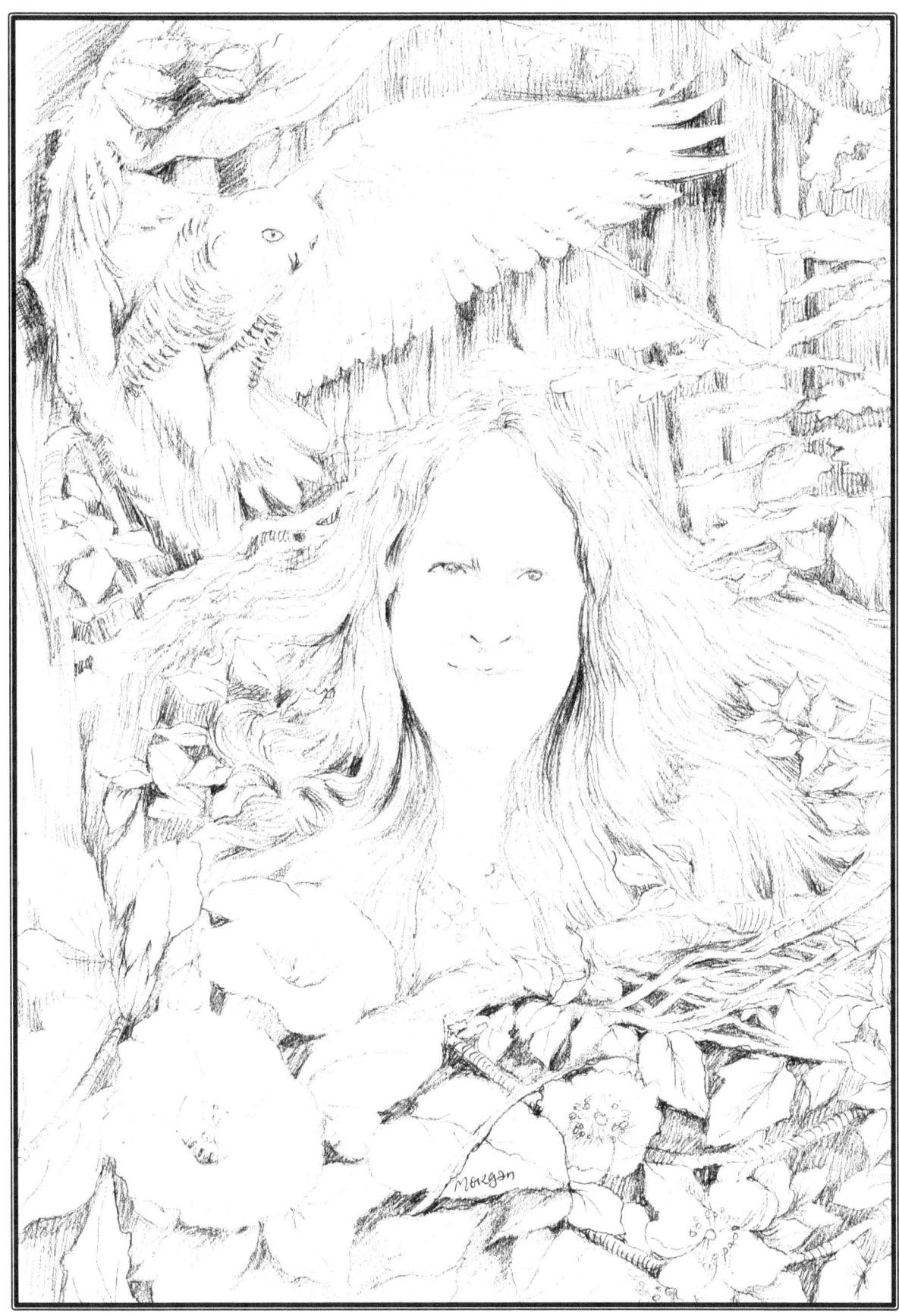

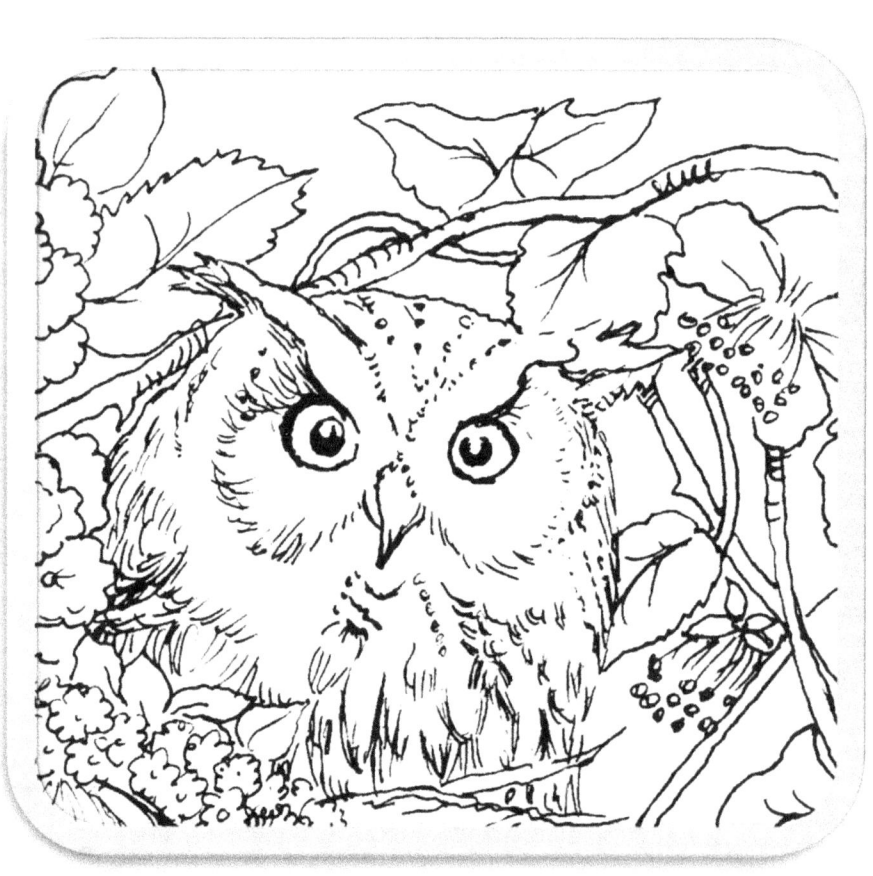

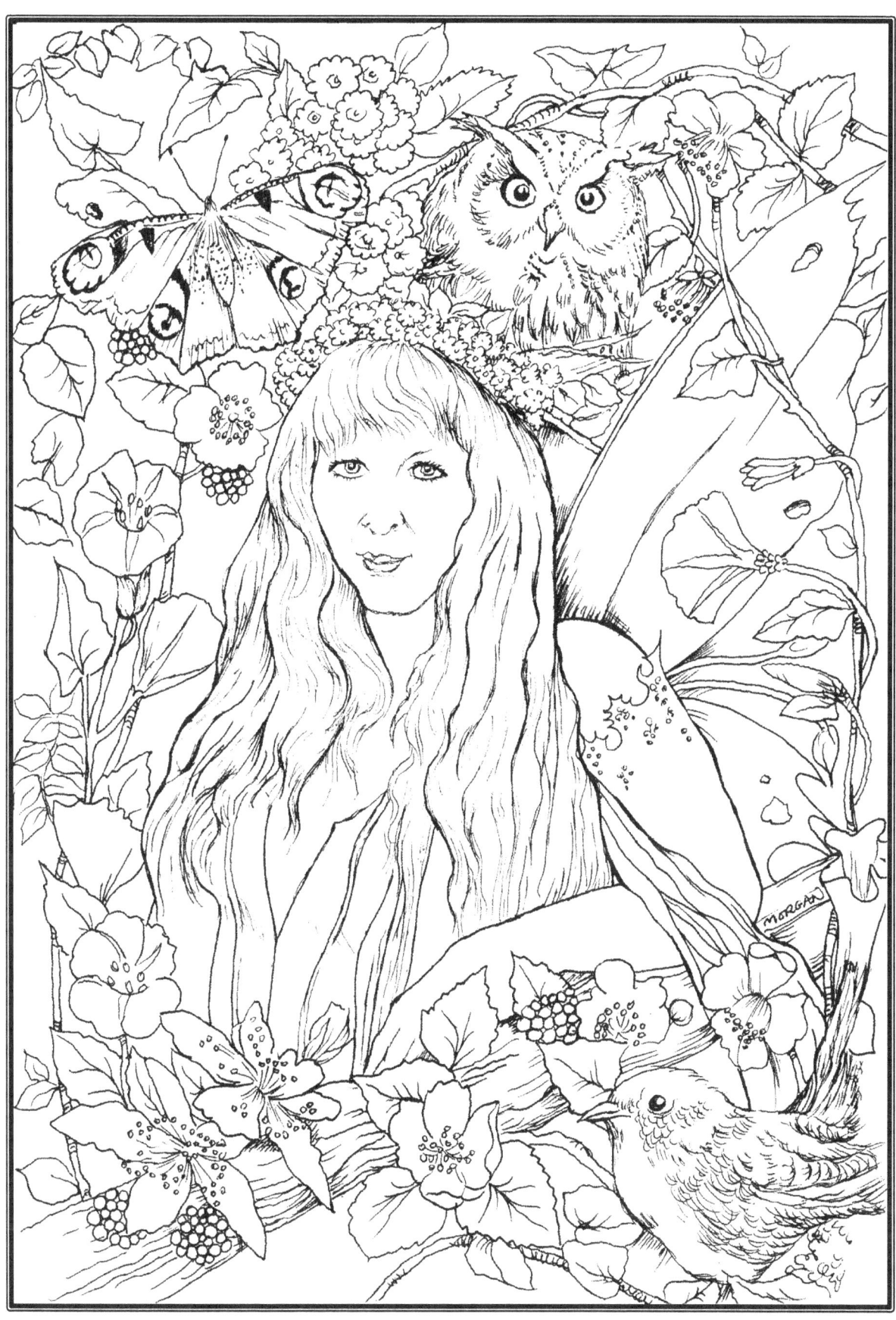

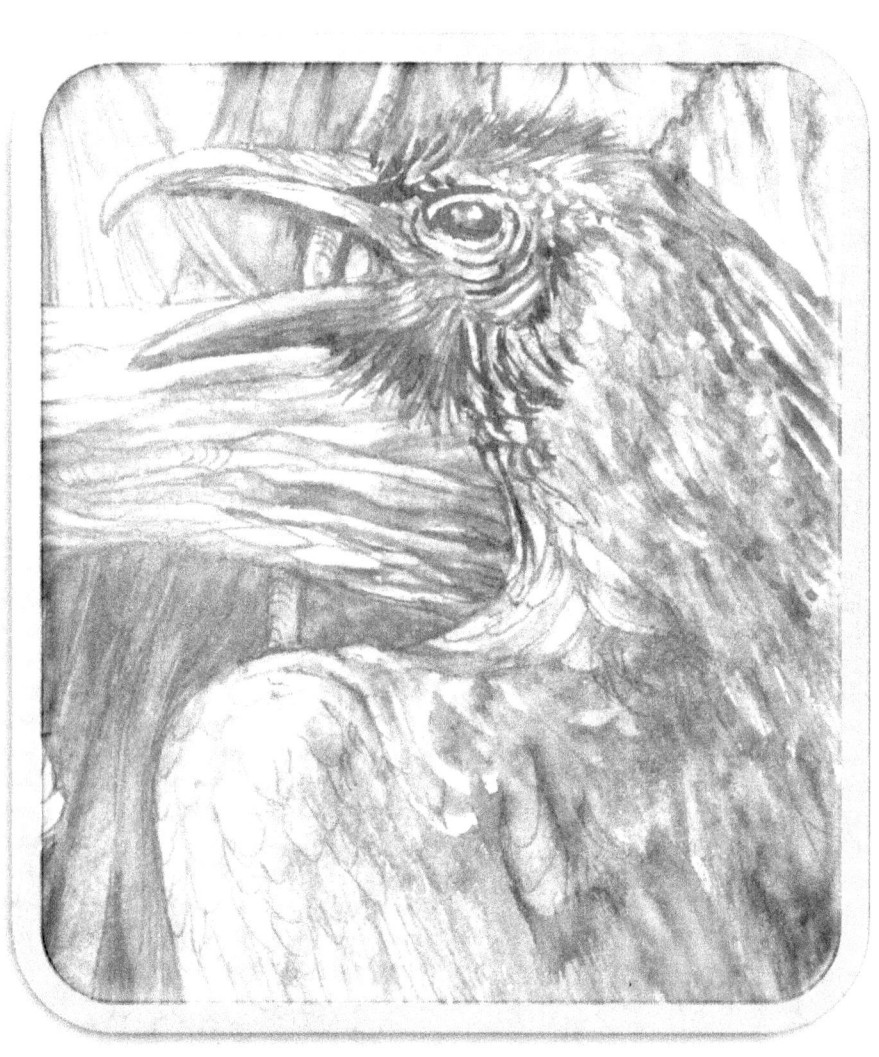

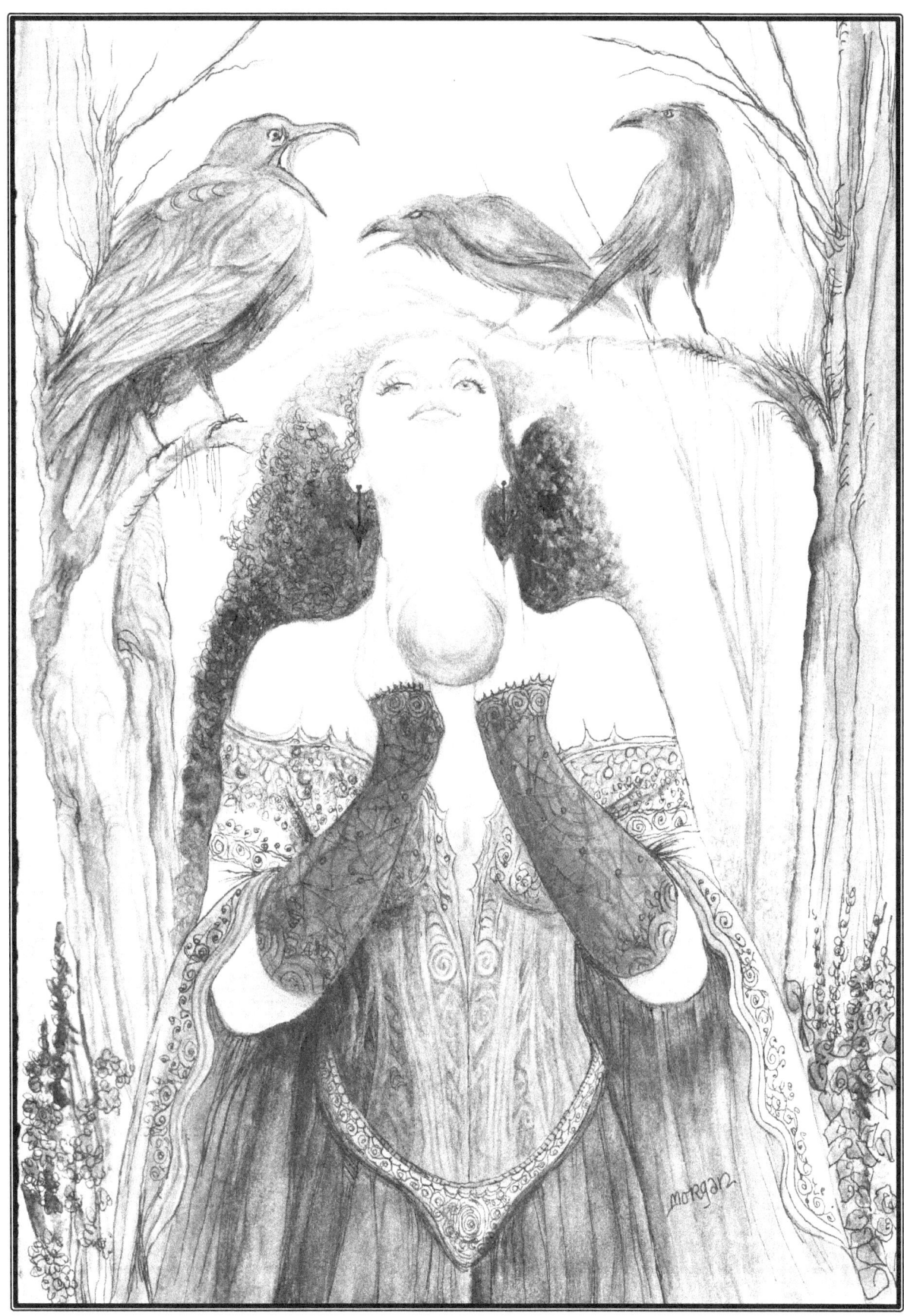

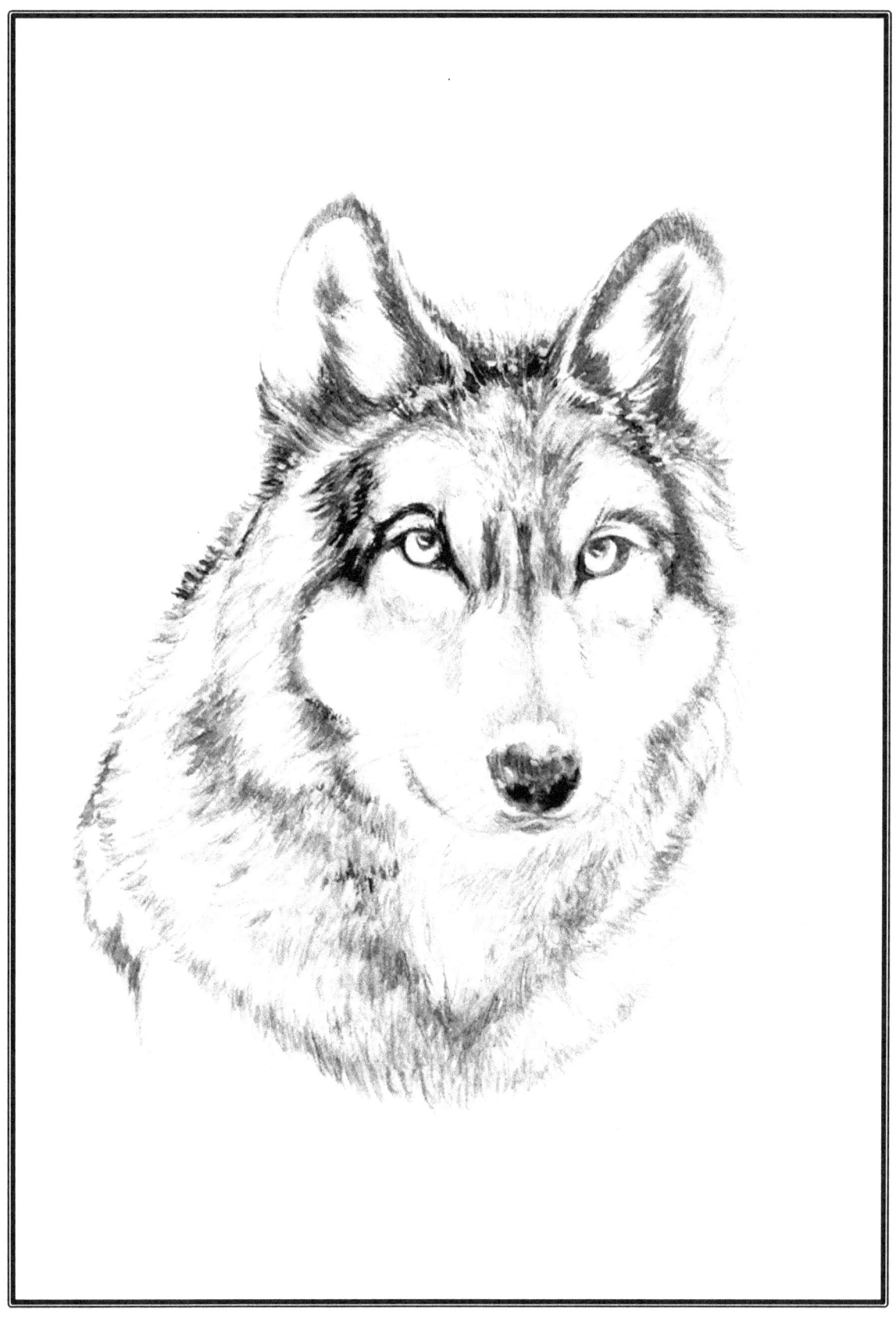

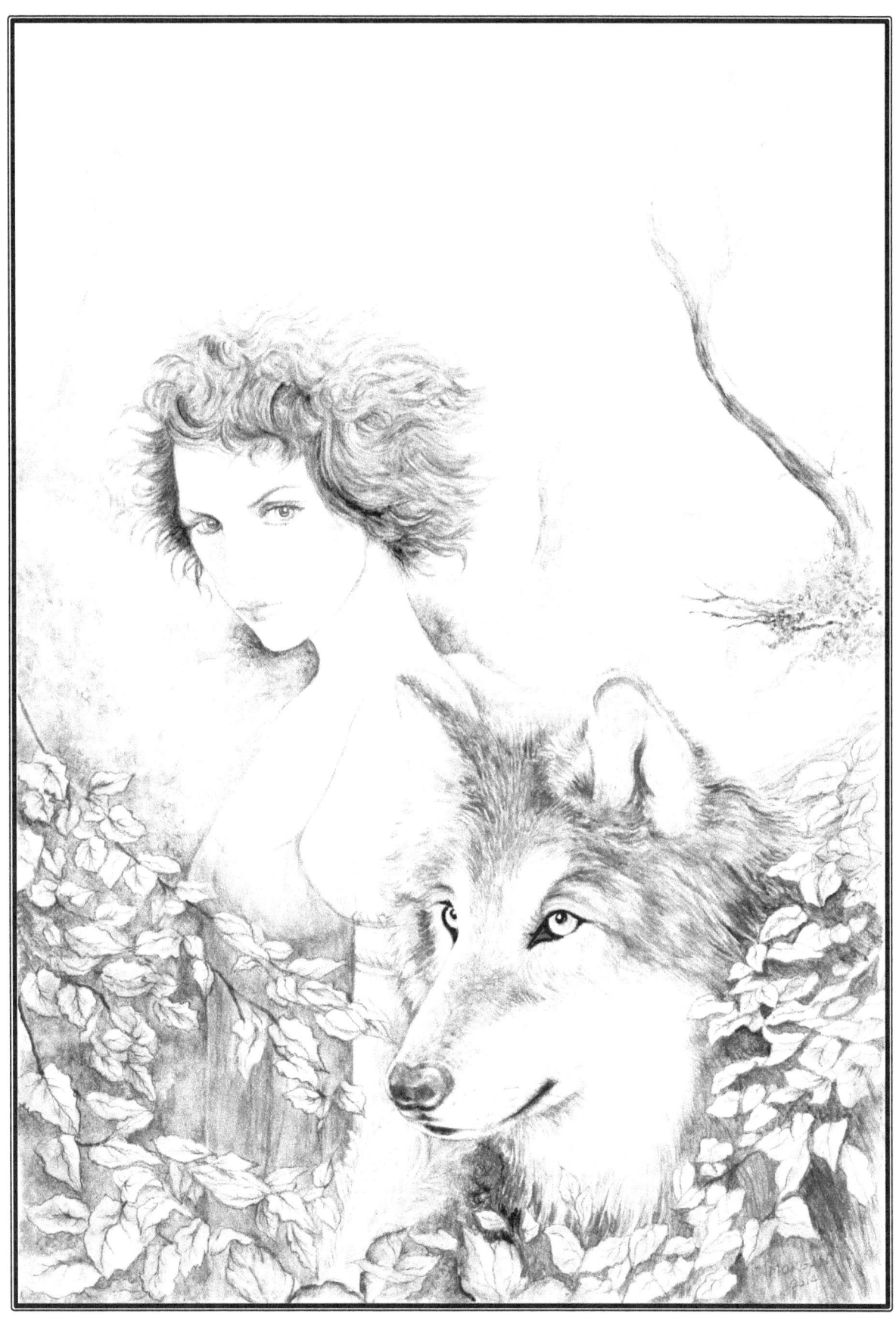

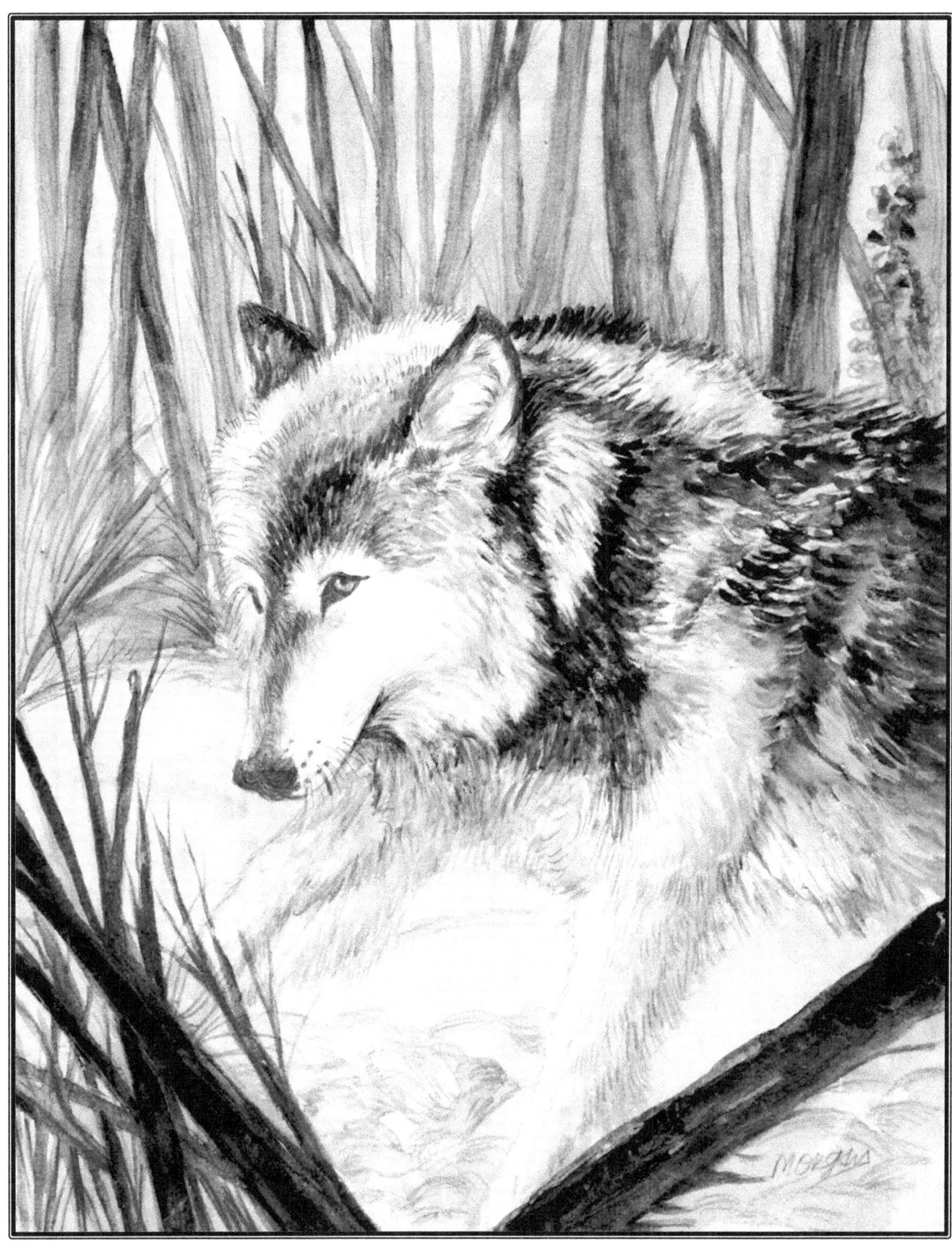

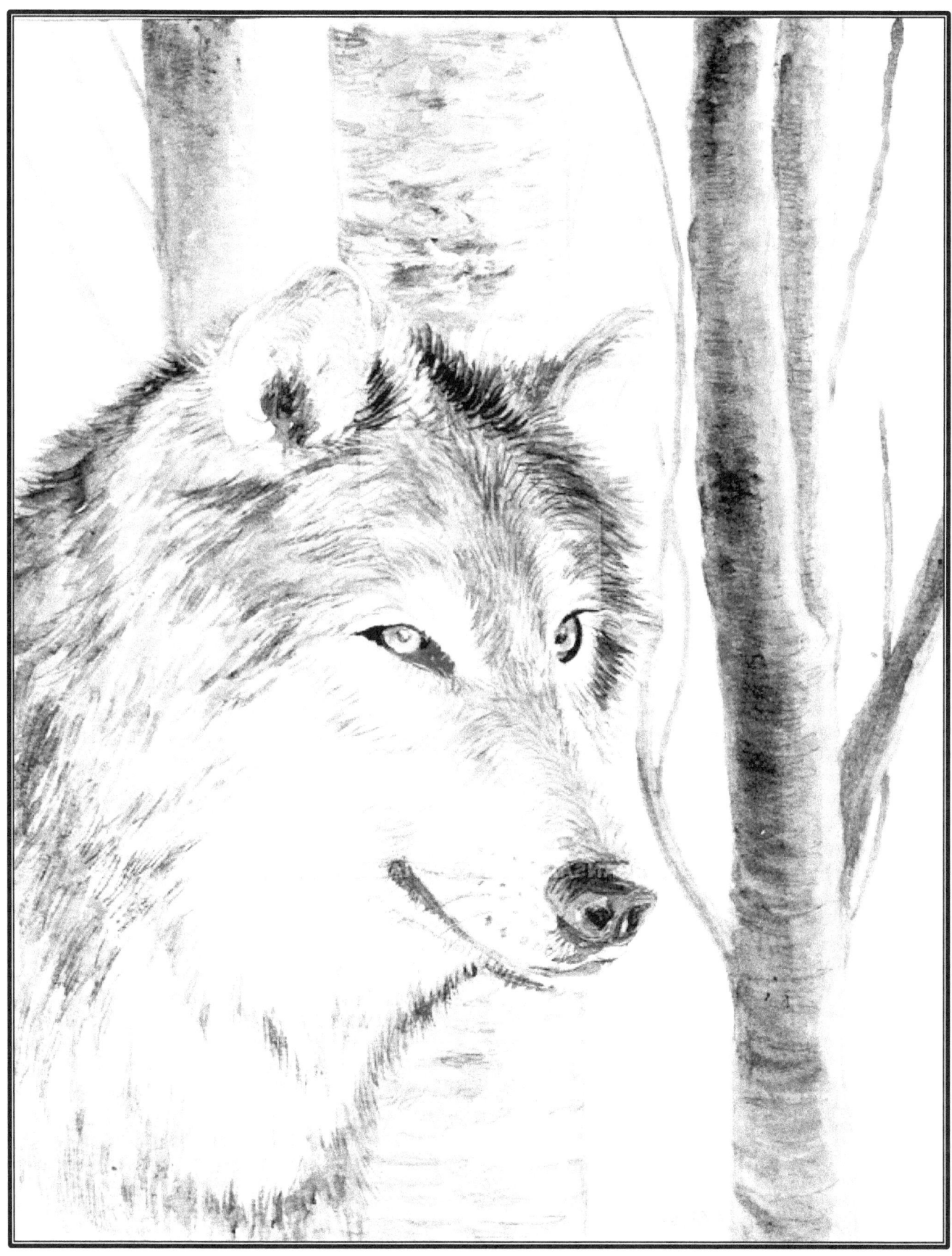

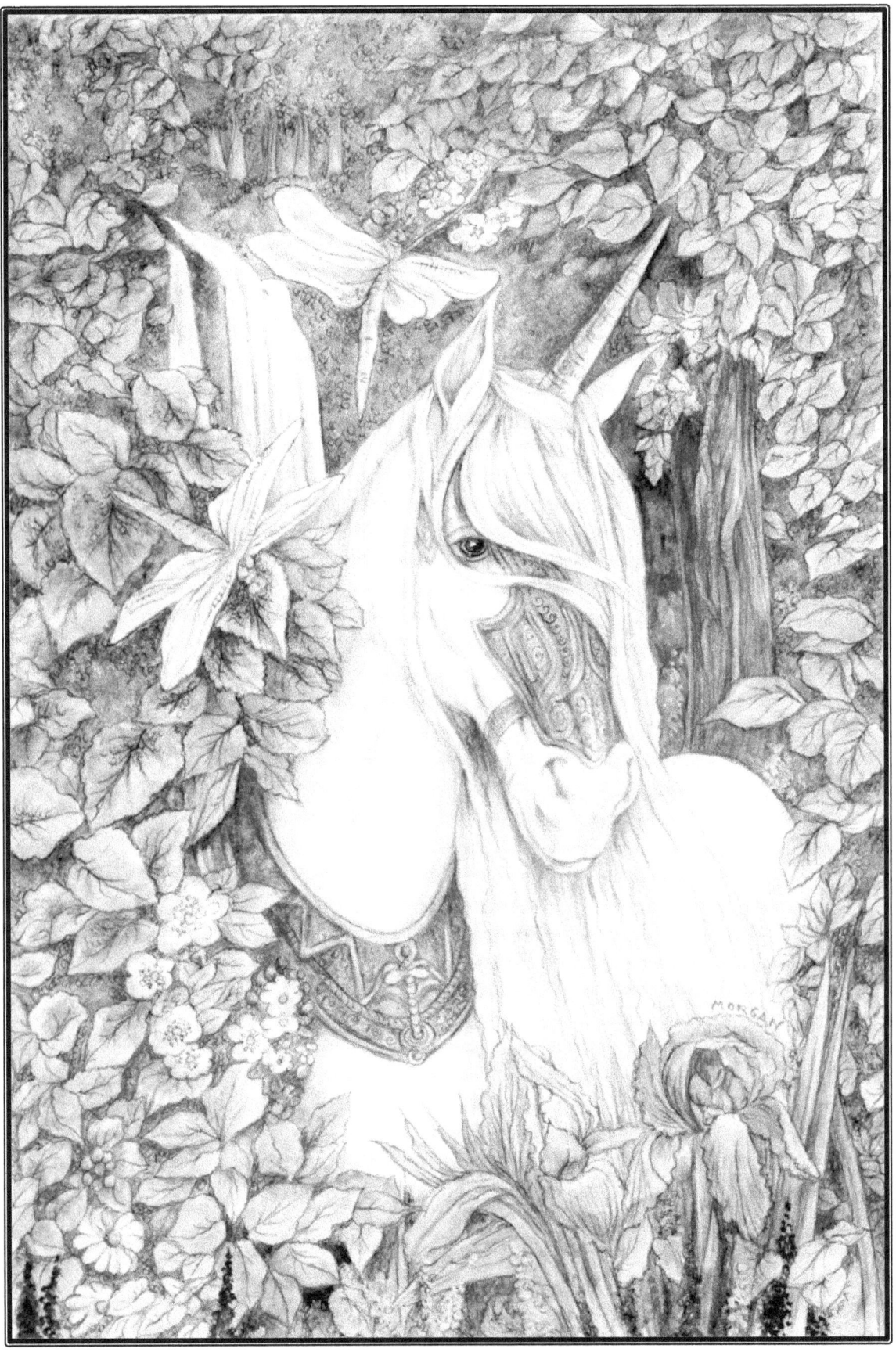

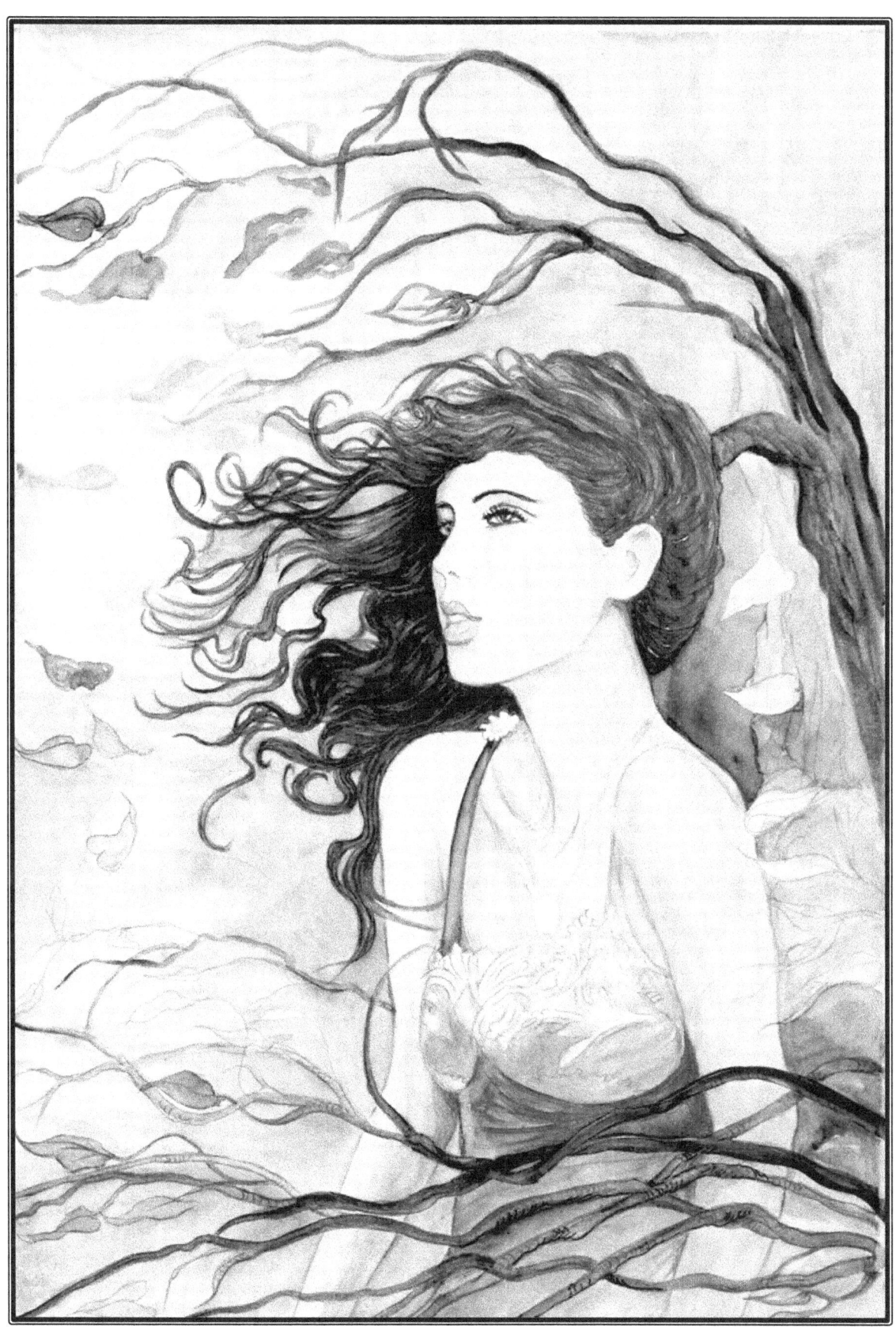

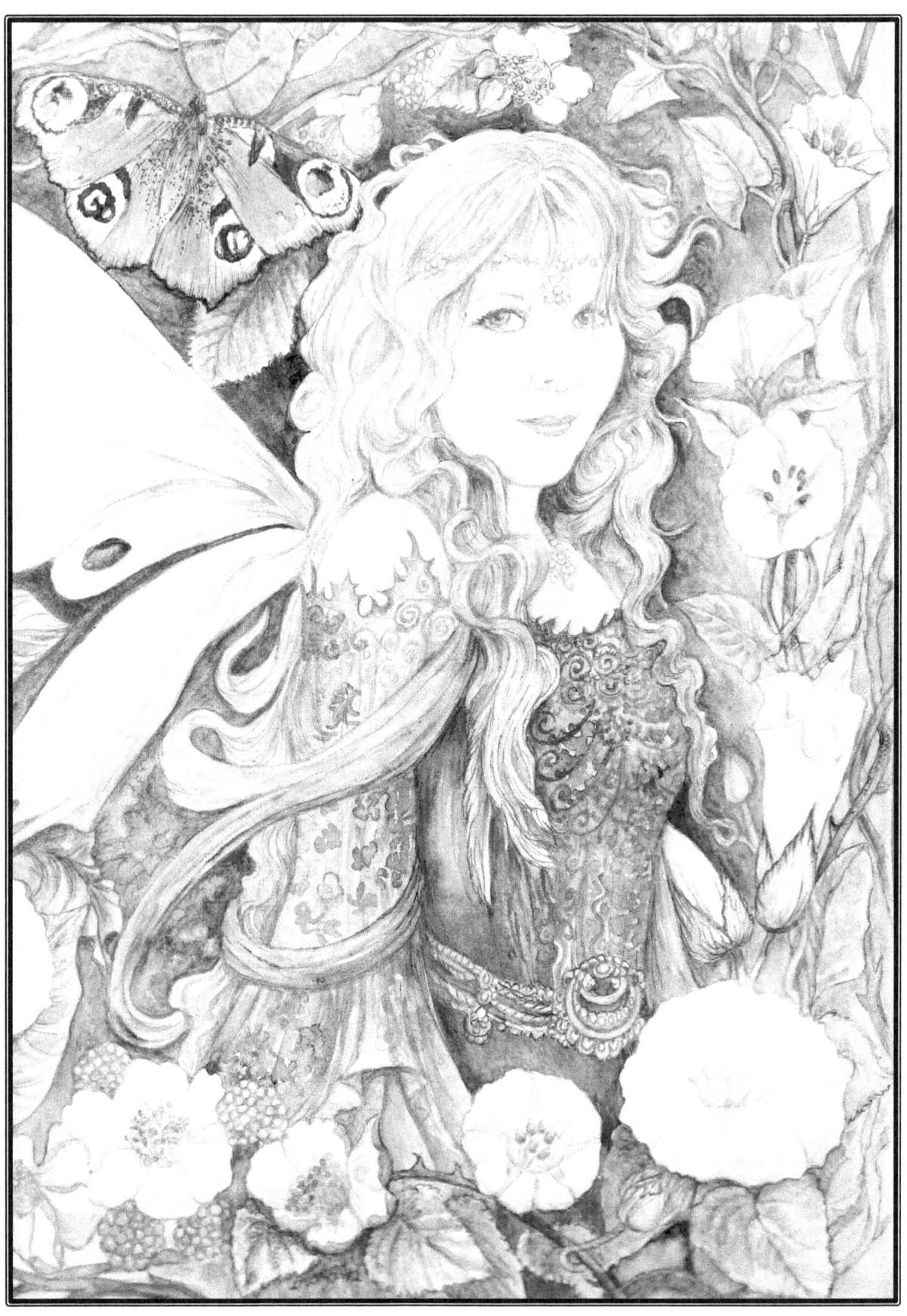

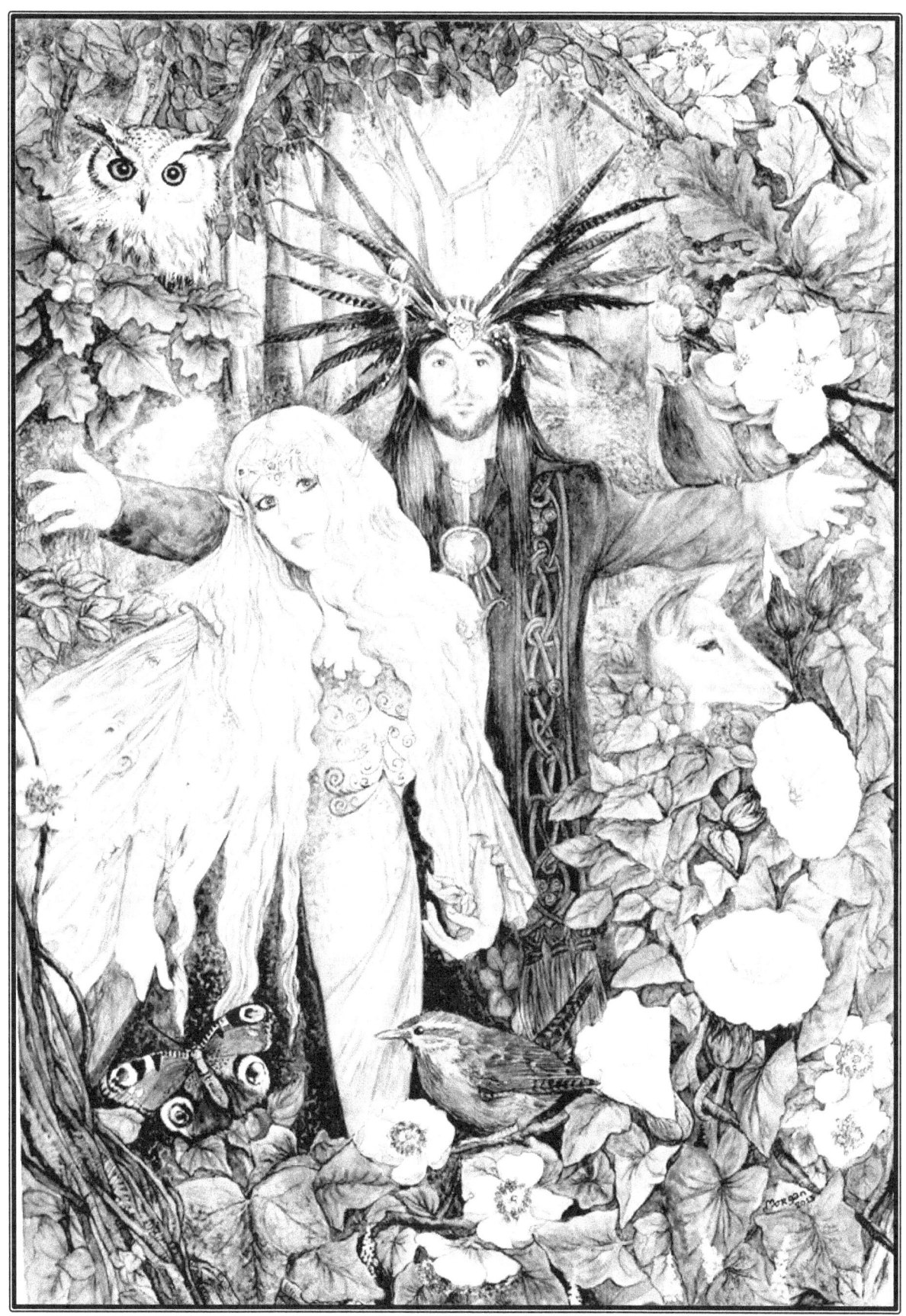

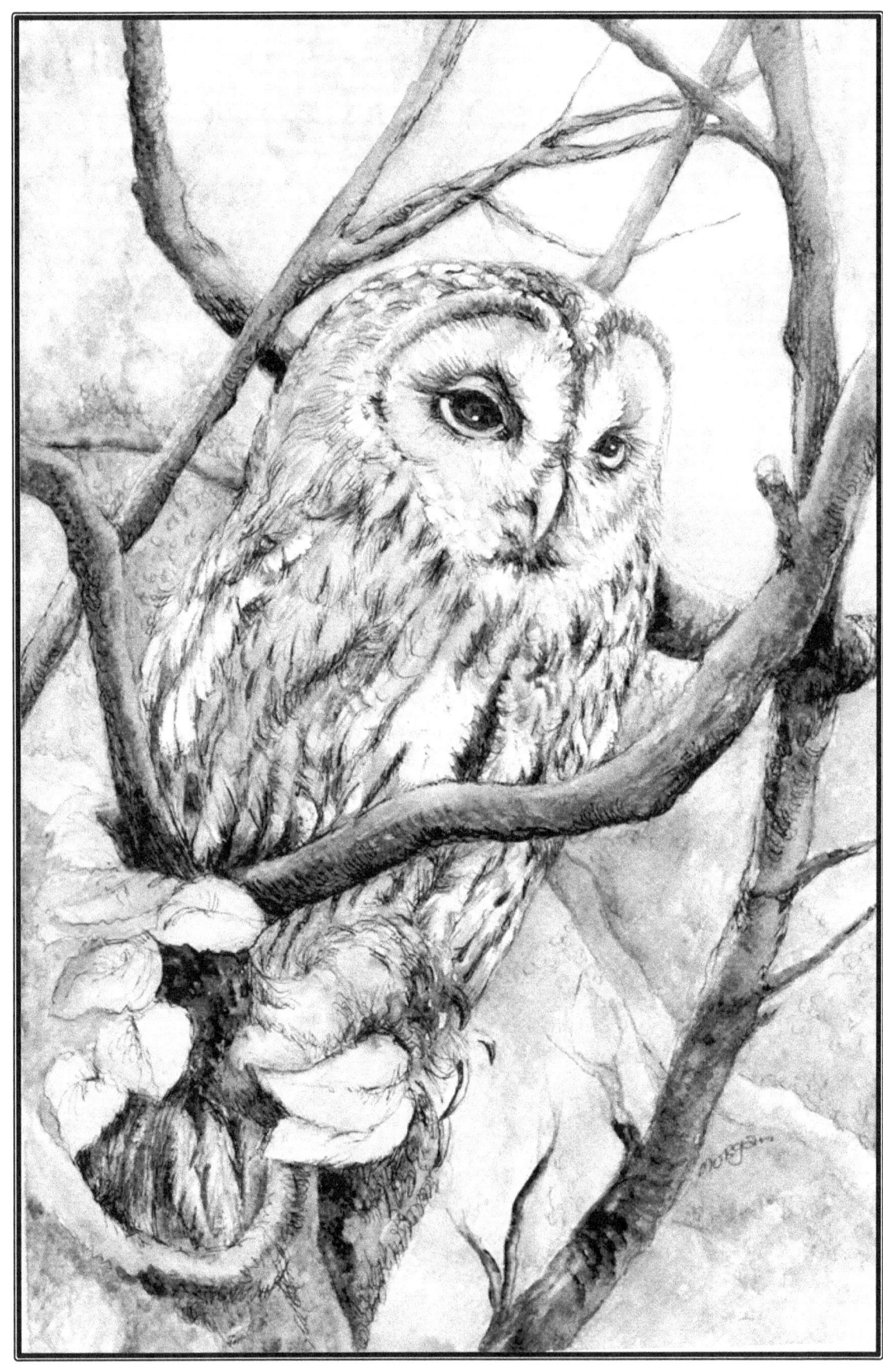

www.ingramcontent.com/pod-product-compliance
Lightning Source LLC
Chambersburg PA
CBHW082257220526
45469CB00009B/3040